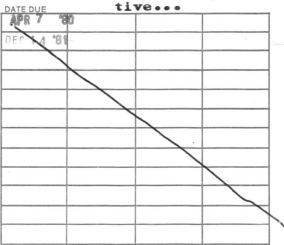

CREATION AND EVOLUTION
IN PRIMITIVE COSMOGONIES

CREATION
AND
EVOLUTION
IN
PRIMITIVE COSMOGONIES

AND OTHER PIECES

BY

SIR JAMES GEORGE FRAZER
O.M., F.R.S., F.B.A.

Essay Index Reprint Series

BOOKS FOR LIBRARIES PRESS, INC.
FREEPORT, NEW YORK

First Published 1935
Reprinted 1967

LIBRARY OF CONGRESS CATALOG CARD NUMBER:

67-26742

PRINTED IN THE UNITED STATES OF AMERICA

ACKNOWLEDGMENTS

A NUMBER of the articles included in this volume have been reprinted from the works in which they originally appeared, and the author wishes to join with his publishers in thanking those who have so kindly given permission for this use of the material : The Cambridge University Press for " Creation and Evolution in Primitive Cosmogonies ", which was first published in *Darwin and Modern Science* under the title of " Some Primitive Theories of the Origin of Man " ; and The Clarendon Press, Oxford, for " Baldwin Spencer as an Anthropologist ", from *Spencer's Last Journey*, and the Zaharoff Lecture for 1933, " Condorcet on the Progress of the Human Mind ". The " Speech on receiving the Freedom of the City of Glasgow " reproduces the text of the address which was privately printed in Glasgow in 1932 at the instance of Mr. G. W. Macfarlane of that city.

PREFACE

ALL but the last of the pieces included in this volume
have appeared in print before, but they are here
collected for the first time. The essay *Creation and
Evolution in Primitive Cosmogonies* was contributed
by me as an article, under the title *Some Primitive
Theories of the Origin of Man*, to the memorial
volume, *Darwin and Modern Science*, which the
Cambridge University Press published in 1909 to
commemorate the fiftieth anniversary of the publication of Darwin's *Origin of Species*. The aim of
the essay is to show that the two hypotheses as
to the origin of man which still divide opinion in
civilized society have been propounded independently
by primitive philosophers at various times and in
various parts of the world. So hard is it for the
human mind even in speculation to strike out an
absolute novelty. Perhaps in the end the two hypotheses may be found to be not so irreconcilable as
at first sight they appear to be. Creative evolution
or evolutionary creation, like the Pre-established
Harmony of Leibniz, may after all be the expression
of that great cosmic process which has wrought,
and is still working, all the wonders of this mysterious
universe, in its majestic progress eternally moulding
the forms and directing the courses alike of atoms and
of stars. Thus it would not be needful to suppose

that in the ordering of the universe the divine is parted from the human by an impassable gulf.

Sir Baldwin Spencer and Canon Roscoe, who are the subjects of two articles in this volume, rendered great and memorable service to the science of man, the one in Australia and the other in Africa. I am proud to have been honoured with their personal friendship and to know that they both believed me to have helped to stimulate and direct their researches. Their books may long survive my own; for a foundation of fact, such as they solidly laid in their writings, is always permanent, while a superstructure of theory is always transitory, being constantly superseded by fresh theories which make nearer and nearer approaches to the truth without ever reaching it. On the shore of the great ocean of reality men are perpetually building theoretical castles of sand, which are perpetually being washed away by the rising tide of knowledge. I cannot expect my own speculations to be more lasting than those of my predecessors. The most that a speculative thinker can hope for is to be remembered for a time as one of the long line of runners, growing dimmer and dimmer as they recede in the distance, who have striven to hand on the torch of knowledge with its little circle of light glimmering in the illimitable darkness of the unknown.

The essay *Condorcet on the Progress of the Human Mind* was delivered as the annual Zaharoff Lecture at Oxford in February 1933 and was afterwards published by the Clarendon Press at Oxford. It develops and expands a former essay of mine on the same subject which was originally published in *The Times Literary Supplement* and is now reprinted in my book *The Gorgon's Head.* The troubled times in which we live, distracted between conflicting ideals, wavering between democracy and despotism, dreaming of universal peace, yet feverishly preparing for universal war, resemble in many respects the stormy times in which Condorcet lived and wrote his famous treatise on the progress of the human mind, and the resemblance adds fresh interest to the proposals which in that work he put forward for remedying some of the evils of his day and hastening the advent of a new and happier era for mankind. Even if from his pages we could glean no practical hints for our guidance, it would still be a gain to escape for a little from the anxieties and forebodings of the present into serene communion with a spirit so lofty and noble as that of Condorcet. Of the literary arts not the least beneficent is that necromancy which can conjure up from the dusty past the spirits of the wise and good who dedicated their genius and their lives to the service of humanity, and by their silent presence can still minister comfort and encouragement to the sad and weary among the living. Of such, we may say in the language of Scripture, is the kingdom of heaven, and of such was Condorcet.

J. G. FRAZER

October 24th, 1934

CONTENTS

		PAGE
I.	CREATION AND EVOLUTION IN PRIMITIVE COSMOGONIES	3
II.	MEDIAEVAL LATIN FABULISTS . . .	37
III.	GIBBON AT LAUSANNE	47
IV.	BALDWIN SPENCER AS ANTHROPOLOGIST . .	55
V.	CANON JOHN ROSCOE	73
VI.	CONDORCET ON THE PROGRESS OF THE HUMAN MIND	83
VII.	SPEECH ON RECEIVING THE FREEDOM OF THE CITY OF GLASGOW	117
VIII.	MEMORIES OF MY PARENTS	131

CREATION AND EVOLUTION IN PRIMITIVE COSMOGONIES

CREATION AND EVOLUTION IN PRIMITIVE COSMOGONIES

On a bright day in late autumn a good many years ago I had ascended the hill of Panopeus in Phocis to examine the ancient Greek fortifications which crest its brow. It was the first of November, but the weather was very hot; and when my work among the ruins was done, I was glad to rest under the shade of a clump of fine holly-oaks, to inhale the sweet refreshing perfume of the wild thyme which scented all the air, and to enjoy the distant prospects, rich in natural beauty, rich too in memories of the legendary and historic past. To the south the finely cut peak of Helicon peered over the low intervening hills. In the west loomed the mighty mass of Parnassus, its middle slopes darkened by pinewoods like shadows of clouds brooding on the mountain-side; while at its skirts nestled the ivy-mantled walls of Daulis overhanging the deep glen, whose romantic beauty accords so well with the loves and sorrows of Procne and Philomela, which Greek tradition associated with the spot. Northwards, across the broad plain to which the hill of Panopeus descends, steep and bare, the eye rested on the gap in the hills through which the Cephissus winds his tortuous way to flow under grey willows, at the foot of barren stony hills, till his turbid waters lose themselves, no longer in the vast reedy swamps of the now vanished Copaic Lake, but in the darkness of a cavern in the limestone rock. Eastward, clinging to the slopes of the bleak range of which the hill of Panopeus forms part, were the ruins of Chaeronea, the birthplace of Plutarch ; and out there in the plain was fought the disastrous battle which laid Greece at the feet of Macedonia. There, too, in a later age East and West met in deadly conflict, when the Roman armies under Sulla defeated the Asiatic hosts of Mithridates. Such was the landscape spread out before me on one of those farewell autumn days of almost pathetic splendour, when the departing summer seems to linger fondly, as if loth to resign to winter the enchanted mountains of Greece. Next day the scene had changed : summer was gone. A grey November mist hung low on the hills which only yesterday had shone resplendent in the sun, and under its melancholy curtain the dead flat of the Chaeronean plain, a wide treeless expanse shut in by desolate slopes, wore an aspect of chilly sadness befitting the battlefield where a nation's freedom was lost.

But crowded as the prospect from Panopeus is with memories of the past, the place itself, now so still and deserted, was once the scene of an event even more ancient and memorable, if Greek story-tellers can be trusted. For here, they say, the sage Prometheus created our first parents by fashioning them, like a potter, out of clay.[1] The very spot where he did so can still be seen. It is a forlorn little glen, or rather hollow, behind the hill of Panopeus, below the ruined but still stately walls and towers which crown the grey rocks of the summit. The glen, when I visited it that hot day after the long drought of summer, was quite dry ; no water trickled down its bushy sides, but in the bottom I found a reddish crumbling earth, a relic perhaps of the clay out of which the potter Prometheus moulded the Greek Adam and Eve. In a volume dedicated to the honour of one who has done more than any other in modern times to shape the ideas of mankind as to their origin, it may not be out of place to recall this crude Greek notion of the creation of the human race, and to compare or contrast it with other rudimentary speculations of primitive peoples on the same subject, if only for the sake of marking the interval which divides the childhood from the maturity of science.

The simple notion that the first man and woman

[1] Pausanias, x. 4. 4. Compare Apollodorus, *Bibliotheca*, i. 7. 1 ; Ovid, *Metamorph.* i. 82 *sq.* ; Juvenal, *Sat.* xiv. 35. According to another version of the tale, this creation of mankind took place not at Panopeus, but at Iconium in Lycaonia. After the original race of mankind had been destroyed in the great flood of Deucalion, the Greek Noah, Zeus commanded Prometheus and Athena to create men afresh by moulding images out of clay, breathing the winds into them, and making them live. See *Etymologicum Magnum*, *s.v.* Ἰκόνιον, pp. 470 *sq.* It is said that Prometheus fashioned the animals as well as men, giving to each kind of beast its proper nature. See Philemon, quoted by Stobaeus, *Florilegium*, ii. 27. The creation of man by Prometheus is figured on ancient works of art. See J. Toutain, *Études de Mythologie et d'Histoire des Religions Antiques* (Paris, 1909), p. 190. According to Hesiod (*Works and Days*, 60 *sqq.*) it was Hephaestus who at the bidding of Zeus moulded the first woman out of moist earth.

B

were modelled out of clay by a god or other super-
human being is found in the traditions of many
peoples. This is the Hebrew belief recorded in
Genesis : " The Lord God formed man of the dust
of the ground, and breathed into his nostrils the
breath of life ; and man became a living soul ".[1]
To the Hebrews this derivation of our species suggested itself all the more naturally because in their
language the word for " ground " (*adamah*) is in
form the feminine of the man (*adam*).[2] From various allusions in Babylonian literature it would seem
that the Babylonians also conceived man to have
been moulded out of clay.[3] According to Berosus,
the Babylonian priest whose account of creation has
been preserved in a Greek version, the god Bel cut
off his own head, and the other gods caught the
flowing blood, mixed it with earth, and fashioned
men out of the bloody paste ; and that, they said, is
why men are so wise, because their mortal clay is
tempered with divine blood.[4] In Egyptian mythology Khnoumou, the father of the gods, is said to
have moulded men out of clay.[5] We cannot doubt
that such crude conceptions of the origin of our race
were handed down to the civilized peoples of antiquity by their savage or barbarous forefathers.
Certainly stories of the same sort are known to be
current among savages and barbarians.

[1] Genesis ii. 7.
[2] S. R. Driver and W. H.
Bennett, in their commentaries
on Genesis ii. 7.
[3] H. Zimmern, in E. Schrader's
*Die Keilinschriften und das Alte
Testament* (Berlin, 1902), p. 506.

[4] Eusebius, *Chronicon*, ed. A.
Schoene, vol. i. (Berlin, 1875),
col. 16.

[5] G. Maspero, *Histoire An-
cienne des Peuples de l'Orient
Classique*, i. (Paris, 1895), p. 128.

Thus the Australian blacks in the neighbourhood of Melbourne said that Pund-jel, the creator, cut three large sheets of bark with his big knife.   On one of these he placed some clay and worked it up with his knife into a proper consistence.   He then laid a portion of the clay on one of the other pieces of bark and shaped it into a human form ; first he made the feet, then the legs, then the trunk, the arms, and the head.   Thus he made a clay man on each of the two pieces of bark ; and being well pleased with them he danced round them for joy. Next he took stringy bark from the eucalyptus-tree, made hair of it, and stuck it on the heads of his clay men.   Then he looked at them again, was pleased with his work, and again danced round them for joy.   He then lay down on them, blew his breath hard into their mouths, their noses, and their navels ; and presently they stirred, spoke, and rose up as full-grown men.[1]   The Maoris of New Zealand say that Tiki made man after his own image.   He took red clay, kneaded it, like the Babylonian Bel, with his own blood, fashioned it in human form, and gave the image breath.   As he had made man in his own likeness he called him *Tiki-ahua* or Tiki's likeness.[2] A very generally received tradition in Tahiti was that the first human pair was made by Taaroa, the

[1] R. Brough Smyth, *The Aborigines of Victoria* (Melbourne, 1878), i. 424.   This and many of the following legends of creation have been already cited by me in a note on Pausanias, x. 4. 4. [*Pausanias's Description of Greece translated with a Commentary* (London, 1898), vol. v. pp. 220 *sq.*]

[2] R. Taylor, *Te Ika A Maui, or New Zealand and its Inhabitants*, Second Edition (London, 1870), p. 117.   Compare E. Shortland, *Maori Religion and Mythology* (London, 1882), pp. 21 *sq.*

chief god. They say that after he had formed the world he created man out of red earth, which was also the food of mankind until bread-fruit was produced. Further, some say that one day Taaroa called for the man by name, and when he came he made him fall asleep. As he slept, the creator took out one of his bones (*ivi*) and made a woman of it, whom he gave to the man to be his wife, and the pair became the progenitors of mankind. This narrative was taken down from the lips of the natives in the early years of the mission to Tahiti. The missionary who records it observes: " This always appeared to me a mere recital of the Mosaic account of creation, which they had heard from some European, and I never placed any reliance on it, although they have repeatedly told me it was a tradition among them before any foreigner arrived. Some have also stated that the woman's name was Ivi, which would be by them pronounced as if written *Eve*. *Ivi* is an aboriginal word, and not only signifies a bone, but also a widow, and a victim slain in war. Notwithstanding the assertion of the natives, I am disposed to think that *Ivi*, or Eve, is the only aboriginal part of the story, as far as it respects the mother of the human race."[1] However, the same tradition has been recorded in other parts of Polynesia besides Tahiti. Thus the natives of Fakaofo or Bowditch Island say that the first man was produced out of a stone. After a time he

[1] W. Ellis, *Polynesian Researches*, Second Edition (London, 1832), i. 110 *sq. Ivi* or *iwi* is the regular word for " bone " in the various Polynesian languages. See E. Tregear, *The Maori-Polynesian Comparative Dictionary* (Wellington, New Zealand, 1891), p. 109.

bethought him of making a woman. So he gathered earth and moulded the figure of a woman out of it, and having done so he took a rib out of his left side and thrust it into the earthen figure, which thereupon started up a live woman. He called her Ivi (Eevee) or " rib " and took her to wife, and the whole human race sprang from this pair.[1] The Maoris also are reported to believe that the first woman was made out of the first man's ribs.[2] This wide diffusion of the story in Polynesia raises a doubt whether it is merely, as Ellis thought, a repetition of the Biblical narrative learned from Europeans. In Nui, or Netherland Island, it was the god Aulialia who made earthen models of a man and woman, raised them up, and made them live. He called the man Tepapa and the woman Tetata.[3]

In the Pelew Islands they say that a brother and sister made men out of clay kneaded with the blood of various animals, and that the characters of these first men and of their descendants were determined by the characters of the animals whose blood had been kneaded with the primordial clay ; for instance, men who have rat's blood in them are thieves, men who have serpent's blood in them are sneaks, and men who have cock's blood in them are brave.[4] According to a Melanesian legend, told in

[1] G. Turner, *Samoa* (London, 1884), pp. 267 *sq.*

[2] J. L. Nicholas, *Narrative of a Voyage to New Zealand* (London, 1817), i. 59, who writes, " and to add still more to this strange coincidence, the general term for bone is *Hevee* ".

[3] G. Turner, *Samoa*, pp. 300 *sq.*

[4] J. Kubary, " Die Religion der Pelauer ", in A. Bastian's *Allerlei aus Volks- und Menschenkunde* (Berlin, 1888), i. 3. 56.

Mota, one of the Banks Islands, the hero Qat moulded men of clay, the red clay from the marshy river-side at Vanua Lava. At first he made men and pigs just alike, but his brothers remonstrated with him, so he beat down the pigs to go on all-fours and made men walk upright. Qat fashioned the first woman out of supple twigs, and when she smiled he knew she was a living woman.[1] A somewhat different version of the Melanesian story is told at Lakona, in Santa Maria. There they say that Qat and another spirit (*vui*) called Marawa both made men. Qat made them out of the wood of dracaena-trees. Six days he worked at them, carving their limbs and fitting them together. Then he allowed them six days to come to life. Three days he hid them away, and three days more he worked to make them live. He set them up and danced to them and beat his drum, and little by little they stirred, till at last they could stand all by themselves. Then Qat divided them into pairs and called each pair husband and wife. Marawa also made men out of a tree, but it was a different tree, the *tavisoviso*. He likewise worked at them six days, beat his drum, and made them live, just as Qat did. But when he saw them move, he dug a pit and buried them in it for six days, and then, when he scraped away the earth to see what they were doing, he found them all rotten and stinking. That was the origin of death.[2]

The inhabitants of Noo-hoo-roa, in the Kei Islands, say that their ancestors were fashioned out

[1] R. H. Codrington, *The Melanesians* (Oxford, 1891), p. 158.

[2] R. H. Codrington, *op. cit.* pp. 157 *sq.*

of clay by the supreme god, Dooadlera, who breathed
life into the clay figures.[1]   The aborigines of Minahassa, in the north of Celebes, say that two beings
called Wailan Wangko and Wangi were alone on
an island, on which grew a cocoanut tree.   Said
Wailan Wangko to Wangi, " Remain on earth while
I climb up the tree".   Said Wangi to Wailan
Wangko, " Good ".   But then a thought occurred
to Wangi and he climbed up the tree to ask Wailan
Wangko why he, Wangi, should remain down there
all alone.   Said Wailan Wangko to Wangi, " Return and take earth and make two images, a man
and a woman ".   Wangi did so, and both images
were men who could move but could not speak.   So
Wangi climbed up the tree to ask Wailan Wangko,
" How now ?   The two images are made, but they
cannot speak."   Said Wailan Wangko to Wangi,
" Take this ginger and go and blow it on the skulls
and the ears of these two images, that they may be
able to speak ; call the man Adam and the woman
Ewa ".[2]   In this narrative the names of the man
and woman betray European influence, but the rest
of the story may be aboriginal.   The Dyaks of
Sakarran in British Borneo say that the first man
was made by two large birds.   At first they tried
to make men out of trees, but in vain.   Then they
hewed them out of rocks, but the figures could not
speak.   Then they moulded a man out of damp
earth and infused into his veins the red gum of the

---

[1] C. M. Pleyte, " Ethnograph-
ische Beschrijving der Kei-Ei-
landen ", *Tijdschrift van het
Nederlandsch Aardrijkskundig*

Genootschap, Tweede Serie, x.
(1893), p. 564.
[2] N. Graafland, *De Minahassa*
(Rotterdam, 1869), i. pp. 96 *sq.*

kumpang-tree. After that they called to him and he answered; they cut him and blood flowed from his wounds.[1]

The Kumis of South-Eastern India related to Captain Lewin, the Deputy-Commissioner of Hill Tracts, the following tradition of the creation of man. " God made the world and the trees and the creeping things first, and after that he set to work to make one man and one woman, forming their bodies of clay ; but each night, on the completion of his work, there came a great snake, which, while God was sleeping, devoured the two images. This happened twice or thrice, and God was at his wits' end, for he had to work all day, and could not finish the pair in less than twelve hours ; besides, if he did not sleep, he would be no good ", said Captain Lewin's informant. " If he were not obliged to sleep, there would be no death, nor would mankind be afflicted with illness. It is when he rests that the snake carries us off to this day. Well, he was at his wits' end, so at last he got up early one morning and first made a dog and put life into it, and that night, when he had finished the images, he set the dog to watch them, and when the snake came, the dog barked and frightened it away. This is the reason at this day that when a man is dying the dogs begin to howl ; but I suppose God sleeps heavily nowadays, or the snake is bolder, for men

[1] Horsburgh, quoted by H. Ling Roth, *The Natives of Sarawak and of British North Borneo* (London, 1896), i. pp. 299 *sq.* Compare the Lord Bishop of Labuan, " On the Wild Tribes of the North-West Coast of Borneo ", *Transactions of the Ethnological Society of London*, New Series, ii. (1863), p. 27.

die all the same."[1] The Khasis of Assam tell a similar tale.[2]

The Ewe-speaking tribes of Togoland, in West Africa, think that God still makes men out of clay. When a little of the water with which he moistens the clay remains over, he pours it on the ground and out of that he makes the bad and disobedient people. When he wishes to make a good man he makes him out of good clay ; but when he wishes to make a bad man, he employs only bad clay for the purpose. In the beginning God fashioned a man and set him on the earth ; after that he fashioned a woman. The two looked at each other and began to laugh, whereupon God sent them into the world.[3] The Innuit or Esquimaux of Point Barrow, in Alaska, tell of a time when there was no man in the land, till a spirit named *á sĕ lu*, who resided at Point Barrow, made a clay man, set him up on the shore to dry, breathed into him and gave him life.[4] Other Esquimaux of Alaska relate how the Raven made the first woman out of clay to be a companion to the first man ; he fastened water-grass to the back of the head to be hair, flapped his wings over the clay figure, and it arose, a beautiful young woman.[5] The Acagchemem Indians of California said that a

---

[1] Capt. T. H. Lewin, *Wild Races of South-Eastern India* (London, 1870), pp. 224-226.

[2] A. Bastian, *Völkerstamme am Brahmaputra und verwandtschaftliche Nachbarn* (Berlin, 1883), p. 8 ; Major P. R. T. Gurdon, *The Khasis* (London, 1907), p. 106.

[3] J. Spieth, *Die Ewe-Stämme, Material zur Kunde des Ewe-Volkes in Deutsch-Togo* (Berlin, 1906), pp. 828, 840.

[4] *Report of the International Expedition to Point Barrow* (Washington, 1885), p. 47.

[5] E. W. Nelson, " The Eskimo about Bering Strait ", *Eighteenth Annual Report of the Bureau of American Ethnology*, Part i. (Washington, 1899), p. 454.

powerful being called Chinigchinich created man out of clay which he found on the banks of a lake ; male and female created he them, and the Indians of the present day are their descendants.[1] A priest of the Natchez Indians in Louisiana told Du Pratz " that God had kneaded some clay, such as that which potters use, and had made it into a little man ; and that after examining it, and finding it well formed, he blew up his work, and forthwith that little man had life, grew, acted, walked, and found himself a man perfectly well shaped ". As to the mode in which the first woman was created, the priest had no information, but thought she was probably made in the same way as the first man ; so Du Pratz corrected his imperfect notions by reference to Scripture.[2] The Michoacans of Mexico said that the great god Tucapacha first made man and woman out of clay, but that when the couple went to bathe in a river they absorbed so much water that the clay of which they were composed all fell to pieces. Then the Creator went to work again and moulded them afresh out of ashes, and after that he essayed a third time and made them of metal. This last attempt succeeded. The metal man and woman bathed in the river without falling to pieces, and by their union they became the pro-genitors of mankind.[3]

[1] Friar Geronimo Boscana, " Chinigchinich ", appended to [A. Robinson's] *Life in California* (New York, 1846), p. 247.
[2] M. Le Page Du Pratz, *The History of Louisiana* (London, 1774), p. 330.

[3] A. de Herrera, *General History of the vast Continent and Islands of America*, translated into English by Capt. J. Stevens (London, 1725, 1726), iii. 254 ; Brasseur de Bourbourg, *Histoire des nations civilisées du Mexique*

According to a legend of the Peruvian Indians,
which was told to a Spanish priest in Cuzco about
half a century after the conquest, it was in Tia-
huanaco that man was first created, or at least was
created afresh after the deluge. " There (in Tia-
huanaco) ", so runs the legend, " the Creator began
to raise up the people and nations that are in that
region, making one of each nation of clay, and
painting the dresses that each one was to wear ;
those that were to wear their hair, with hair, and
those that were to be shorn, with hair cut. And to
each nation was given the language that was to be
spoken, and the songs to be sung, and the seeds and
food that they were to sow. When the Creator had
finished painting and making the said nations and
figures of clay, he gave life and soul to each one, as
well men as women, and ordered that they should
pass under the earth. Thence each nation came up
in the places to which he ordered them to go." [1]

These examples suffice to prove that the theory
of the creation of man out of dust or clay has been
current among savages in many parts of the world.
But it is by no means the only explanation which the
savage philosopher has given of the beginnings of
human life on earth. Struck by the resemblances
which may be traced between himself and the beasts,
he has often supposed, like Darwin himself, that
mankind has been developed out of lower forms of
animal life. For the simple savage has none of that
high notion of the transcendent dignity of man

et de l'Amérique-Centrale (Paris,
1857–1859), iii. 80 *sq.* ; compare
id., i. 54 *sq.*

[1] E. J. Payne, *History of the
New World called America*, i.
(Oxford, 1892), p. 462.

which makes so many superior persons shrink with horror from the suggestion that they are distant cousins of the brutes. He on the contrary is not too proud to own his humble relations; indeed his difficulty often is to perceive the distinction between him and them. Questioned by a missionary, a Bushman of more than average intelligence "could not state any difference between a man and a brute— he did not know but a buffalo might shoot with bows and arrows as well as a man, if it had them ".[1] When the Russians first landed on one of the Alaskan islands, the natives took them for cuttle-fish " on account of the buttons on their clothes ".[2] The Giliaks of the Amoor think that the outward form and size of an animal are only apparent; in substance every beast is a real man, just like a Giliak himself, only endowed with an intelligence and strength which often surpass those of mere ordinary human beings.[3] The Borororos, an Indian tribe of Brazil, will have it that they are parrots of a gorgeous red plumage which live in their native forests. Accordingly, they treat the birds as their fellow-tribesmen, keeping them in captivity, refusing to eat their flesh, and mourning for them when they die.[4]

This sense of the close relationship of man to the lower creation is the essence of totemism, that curi-

---

[1] Rev. John Campbell, *Travels in South Africa* (London, 1822), ii. p. 34.

[2] I. Petroff, *Report on the Population, Industries, and Resources of Alaska*, p. 145.

[3] L. Sternberg, " Die Religion der Giljaken ", *Archiv für Religionswissenschaft*, viii. (1905), p. 248.

[4] K. von den Steinen, *Unter den Naturvölkern Zentral-Brasiliens* (Berlin, 1894), pp. 352 *sq.*, 512.

ous system of superstition which unites by a mystic
bond a group of human kinsfolk to a species of
animals or plants.   Where that system exists in full
force, the members of a totem clan identify themselves with their totem animals in a way and to an
extent which we find it hard even to imagine.   For
example, men of the Cassowary clan in Mabuiag
think that cassowaries are men or nearly so.
" Cassowary, he all same as relation, he belong same
family ", is the account they give of their relationship with the long-legged bird.   Conversely they
hold that they themselves are cassowaries for all
practical purposes.   They pride themselves on having long thin legs like a cassowary.   This reflection
affords them peculiar satisfaction when they go out
to fight, or to run away, as the case may be ; for at
such times a Cassowary man will say to himself,
" My leg is long and thin, I can run and not feel
tired ; my legs will go quickly and the grass will not
entangle them ".   Members of the Cassowary clan
are reputed to be pugnacious, because the cassowary
is a bird of very uncertain temper and can kick with
extreme violence.[1]   So among the Ojibways men
of the Bear clan are reputed to be surly and pugnacious like bears, and men of the Crane clan to
have clear ringing voices like cranes.[2]   Hence the
savage will often speak of his totem animal as his

[1] A. C. Haddon, " The Ethno-
graphy of the Western Tribe of
Torres Straits ", *Journal of the
Anthropological Institute*, xix.
(1890), p. 309 ; *Reports of the
Cambridge Anthropological Expedition to Torres Straits*, v.

(Cambridge, 1904), pp. 166, 184.

[2] W. W. Warren, " History of
the Ojibways ", *Collections of the
Minnesota Historical Society*, v.
(Saint Paul, Minn., 1885), pp.
47, 49.

father or his brother, and will neither kill it himself
nor allow others to do so, if he can help it. For
example, if somebody were to kill a bird in the
presence of a native Australian who had the bird
for his totem, the black might say, " What for you
kill that fellow ? that my father ! " or " That
brother belonging to me you have killed ; why did
you do it ? " [1] Bechuanas of the Porcupine clan
are greatly afflicted if anybody hurts or kills a porcupine in their presence. They say, " They have
killed our brother, our master, one of ourselves, him
whom we sing of " ; and so saying they piously
gather the quills of their murdered brother, spit on
them, and rub their eyebrows with them. They
think they would die if they touched its flesh. In
like manner Bechuanas of the Crocodile clan call
the crocodile one of themselves, their master, their
brother ; and they mark the ears of their cattle
with a long slit like a crocodile's mouth by way of a
family crest. Similarly, Bechuanas of the Lion clan
would not, like the members of other clans, partake
of lion's flesh ; for how, say they, could they eat
their grandfather ? If they are forced in self-
defence to kill a lion, they do so with great regret
and rub their eyes carefully with its skin, fearing to
lose their sight if they neglected this precaution.[2]
A Mandingo porter has been known to offer the
whole of his month's pay to save the life of a python,
because the python was his totem and he therefore

[1] E. Palmer, " Notes on some   *Relation d'un voyage d'explora-*
Australian Tribes ", *Journal of*   *tion au Nord-Est de la Colonie*
the Anthropological Institute, xiii.   *du Cap de Bonne - Espérance*
(1884), p. 300.   (Paris, 1842), pp. 349 *sq.*, 422-
[2] T. Arbousset et F. Daumas,   424.

regarded the reptile as his relation ; he thought that if he allowed the creature to be killed, the whole of his own family would perish, probably through the vengeance to be taken by the reptile kinsfolk of the murdered serpent.[1]

Sometimes, indeed, the savage goes further and identifies the revered animal not merely with a kinsman but with himself ; he imagines that one of his own more or less numerous souls, or at all events that a vital part of himself, is in the beast, so that if it is killed he must die.   Thus, the Balong tribe of the Cameroons, in West Africa, think that every man has several souls, of which one is lodged in an elephant, a wild boar, a leopard, or what not. When any one comes home, feels ill, and says, " I shall soon die ", and is as good as his word, his friends are of opinion that one of his souls has been shot by a hunter in a wild boar or a leopard, for example, and that that is the real cause of his death.[2]   A Catholic missionary, sleeping in the hut of a chief of the Fan negroes, awoke in the middle of the night to see a huge black serpent of the most dangerous sort in the act of darting at him.   He was about to shoot it when the chief stopped him, saying, " In killing that serpent, it is me that you would have killed.   Fear nothing, the serpent is my *elangela.*" [3]   At Calabar there used to be some

---

[1] M. le Docteur Tautain, " Notes sur les croyances et pratiques religieuses des Banmanas ", *Revue d'Ethnographie,* iii. (1885), pp. 396 *sq.* ; A. Rançon, *Dans la Haute-Gambie, Voyage d'exploration scientifique* (Paris, 1894), p. 445.

[2] J. Keller, " Ueber das Land und Volk der Balong ", *Deutsches Kolonialblatt,* 1 Oktober 1895, p. 484.

[3] Father Trilles, " Chez les Fang, leurs Moeurs, leur Langue, leur Religion ", *Les Missions Catholiques,* xxx. (1898), p. 322.

years ago a huge old crocodile which was well
known to contain the spirit of a chief who resided
in the flesh at Duke Town.   Sporting Vice-Consuls,
with a reckless disregard of human life, from time to
time made determined attempts to injure the animal,
and once a peculiarly active officer succeeded in
hitting it.   The chief was immediately laid up with
a wound in his leg.   He *said* that a dog had bitten
him, but few people perhaps were deceived by so
flimsy a pretext.[1]   Once when Mr. Partridge's
canoe-men were about to catch fish near an Assiga
town in Southern Nigeria, the natives of the town
objected, saying, " Our souls live in those fish, and
if you kill them we shall die ".[2]   On another occasion, in the same region, an Englishman shot a
hippopotamus near a native village.   The same
night a woman died in the village, and her friends
demanded and obtained from the marksman five
pounds as compensation for the murder of the
woman, whose soul or second self had been in that
hippopotamus.[3]   Similarly at Ndolo, in the Congo
region, we hear of a chief whose life was bound up
with a hippopotamus, but he prudently suffered no
one to fire at the animal.[4]

[1] Miss Mary H. Kingsley,
Travels in West Africa (London,
1897), pp. 538 *sq.* As to the
external or bush souls of human
beings, which in this part of
Africa are supposed to be lodged
in the bodies of animals, see Miss
Mary H. Kingsley, *op. cit.* pp.
459-461 ; R. Henshaw, " Notes
on the Efik belief in ' bush soul ' ",
Man, vi. (1906), pp. 121 *sq.* ; J.
Parkinson, " Notes on the Asaba

People (Ibos) of the Niger ",
*Journal of the Anthropological
Institute*, xxxvi. (1906), pp. 314 *sq.*
[2] Charles Partridge, *Cross
River Natives* (London, 1905),
pp. 225 *sq.*
[3] C. H. Robinson, *Hausaland*
(London, 1896), pp. 36 *sq.*
[4] *Notes Analytiques sur les
Collections Ethnographiques du
Musée du Congo*, i. (Brussels,
1902–1906), p. 150.

Amongst people who thus fail to perceive any sharp line of distinction between beasts and men it is not surprising to meet with the belief that human beings are directly descended from animals. Such a belief is often found among totemic tribes who imagine that their ancestors sprang from their totemic animals or plants ; but it is by no means confined to them. Thus, to take instances, some of the Californian Indians, in whose mythology the coyote or prairie-wolf is a leading personage, think that they are descended from coyotes. At first they walked on all-fours ; then they began to have some members of the human body, one finger, one toe, one eye, one ear, and so on ; then they got two fingers, two toes, two eyes, two ears, and so forth ; till at last, progressing from period to period, they became perfect human beings. The loss of their tails, which they still deplore, was produced by the habit of sitting upright.[1] Similarly, Darwin thought that " the tail has disappeared in man and the anthropomorphous apes, owing to the terminal portion having been injured by friction during a long lapse of time ; the basal and embedded portion having been reduced and modified, so as to become suitable to the erect or semi-erect position ".[2] The Turtle clan of the Iroquois think that they are descended from real mud turtles which used to live in a pool. One hot summer the pool dried up, and the mud

[1] H. R. Schoolcraft, *Indian Tribes of the United States*, iv. (Philadelphia, 1856), pp. 224 *sq.* ; compare *id.*, v. p. 217. The descent of some, not all, Indians from coyotes is mentioned also by Friar Boscana, in [A. Robinson's] *Life in California* (New York, 1846), p. 299.

[2] Charles Darwin, *The Descent of Man*, Second Edition (London, 1875), p. 60.

turtles set out to find another. A very fat turtle, waddling after the rest in the heat, was much incommoded by the weight of his shell, till by a great effort he heaved it off altogether. After that he gradually developed into a man and became the progenitor of the Turtle clan.[1] The Crawfish band of the Choctaws are in like manner descended from real crawfish, which used to live under ground, only coming up occasionally through the mud to the surface. Once a party of Choctaws smoked them out, taught them the Choctaw languages, taught them to walk on two legs, made them cut off their toe-nails and pluck the hair from their bodies, after which they adopted them into the tribe. But the rest of their kindred, the crawfish, are crawfish under ground to this day.[2] The Osage Indians universally believed that they were descended from a male snail and a female beaver. A flood swept the snail down to the Missouri and left him high and dry on the bank, where the sun ripened him into a man. He met and married a beaver maid, and from the pair the tribe of the Osages is descended. For a long time these Indians retained a pious reverence for their animal ancestors and refrained from hunting beavers, because in killing a beaver they killed a brother of the Osages. But when white men came among them and offered high prices for beaver skins, the Osages yielded to the temptation and took the lives of their furry brethren.[3] The Carp clan of the

[1] E. A. Smith, " Myths of the Iroquois", *Second Annual Report of the Bureau of Ethnology* (Washington, 1883), p. 77.

[2] Geo. Catlin, *North American Indians* (London, 1844), ii. p. 128.

[3] Lewis and Clarke, *Travels to the Source of the Missouri River* (London, 1815), i. 12 (vol. i. pp. 44 *sq.* of the London reprint, 1905).

Ootawak Indians are descended from the eggs of a carp which had been deposited by the fish on the banks of a stream and warmed by the sun.[1] The Crane clan of the Ojibways are sprung originally from a pair of cranes, which after long wanderings settled on the rapids at the outlet of Lake Superior, where they were changed by the Great Spirit into a man and woman.[2] The members of two Omaha clans were originally buffaloes and lived, oddly enough, under water, which they splashed about, making it muddy.   And at death all the members of these clans went back to their ancestors the buffaloes. So when one of them lay a-dying, his friends used to wrap him up in a buffalo skin with the hair outside and say to him, " You came hither from the animals and you are going back thither.   Do not face this way again.   When you go, continue walking." [3] The Haida Indians of Queen Charlotte Islands believe that long ago the raven, who is the chief figure in the mythology of North-West America, took a cockle from the beach and married it ; the cockle gave birth to a female child, whom the raven took to wife, and from their union the Indians were produced.[4] The Delaware Indians called the rattlesnake their grandfather and would on no account destroy one of these reptiles, believing that were they to do so the whole race of rattlesnakes would rise up

[1] *Lettres Édifiantes et Curieuses*, Nouvelle Édition, vi. (Paris, 1781), p. 171.

[2] L. H. Morgan, *Ancient Society* (London, 1877), p. 180.

[3] J. Owen Dorsey, " Omaha Sociology ", *Third Annual Report of the Bureau of Ethno-*logy (Washington, 1844), pp. 229, 233.

[4] G. M. Dawson, *Report on the Queen Charlotte Islands* (Montreal, 1880), pp. 149 B *sq.* (*Geological Survey of Canada*) ; F. Poole, *Queen Charlotte Islands*, p. 136.

and bite them. Under the influence of the white man, however, their respect for their grandfather the rattlesnake gradually died away, till at last they killed him without compunction or ceremony whenever they met him. The writer who records the old custom observes that he had often reflected on the curious connexion which appears to subsist in the mind of an Indian between man and the brute creation ; " all animated nature," says he, " in whatever degree, is in their eyes a great whole, from which they have not yet ventured to separate themselves."[1]

Some of the Indians of Peru boasted of being descended from the puma or American lion ; hence they adored the lion as a god and appeared at festivals like Hercules dressed in the skins of lions with the heads of the beasts fixed over their own. Others claimed to be sprung from condors and attired themselves in great black and white wings, like that enormous bird.[2] The Wanika of East Africa look upon the hyaena as one of their ancestors or as associated in some way with their origin and destiny. The death of a hyaena is mourned by the whole people, and the greatest funeral ceremonies which they perform are performed for this brute. The wake held over a chief is as nothing compared to the wake held over a hyaena ; one tribe only

[1] Rev. John Heckewelder, " An Account of the History, Manners and Customs of the Indian Nations, who once inhabited Pennsylvania and the Neighbouring States ", *Transactions of the Historical and Literary Committee of the Ameri-* *can Philosophical Society*, i. (Philadelphia, 1819), pp. 245, 247, 248.

[2] Garcilasso de la Vega, *First Part of the Royal Commentaries of the Yncas*, vol. i. p. 323, vol. ii. p. 156 (Markham's translation).

mourns the death of its chief, but all the tribes unite
to celebrate the obsequies of a hyaena.[1] Some
Malagasy families claim to be descended from the
babacoote (*Lichanotus brevicaudatus*), a large lemur
of grave appearance and staid demeanour, which
lives in the depth of the forest. When they find
one of these creatures dead, its human descendants
bury it solemnly, digging a grave for it, wrapping
it in a shroud, and weeping and lamenting over its
carcase. A doctor who had shot a babacoote was
accused by the inhabitants of a Betsimisaraka village
of having killed " one of their grandfathers in the
forest ", and to appease their indignation he had to
promise not to skin the animal in the village but
in a solitary place where nobody could see him.[2]
Many of the Betsimisaraka believe that the curious
nocturnal animal called the aye-aye (*Cheiromys
madagascariensis*) " is the embodiment of their forefathers, and hence will not touch it, much less do it
an injury. It is said that when one is discovered
dead in the forest, these people make a tomb for it
and bury it with all the forms of a funeral. They
think that if they attempt to entrap it they will
surely die in consequence." [3] Some Malagasy

[1] Charles New, *Life, Wanderings, and Labours in Eastern
Africa* (London, 1873), p. 122.
[2] Father Abinal, " Croyances
fabuleuses des Malgaches ", *Les
Missions Catholiques*, xii. (1880),
p. 526 ; G. H. Smith, " Some
Betsimisaraka Superstitions", *The
Antananarivo Annual and Mada-
gascar Magazine*, No. 10 (Antan-
anarivo, 1886) p. 239; H. W. Little,
Madagascar, its History and
People (London, 1884), pp. 321
sq. ; A. van Gennep, *Tabou et
Totémisme à Madagascar* (Paris,
1904), pp. 214 *sqq.*
[3] G. A. Shaw, " The Aye-
aye ", *Antananarivo Annual and
Madagascar Magazine*, vol. ii.
(Antananarivo, 1896), pp. 201,
203 (Reprint of the Second four
Numbers). Compare A. van
Gennep, *Tabou et Totémisme à
Madagascar*, pp. 223 *sq.*

tribes believe themselves descended from crocodiles and accordingly they deem the formidable
reptiles their brothers. If one of these scaly brothers
so far forgets the ties of kinship as to devour a man,
the chief of the tribe, or in his absence an old man
familiar with the tribal customs, repairs at the head
of the people to the edge of the water, and summons
the family of the culprit to deliver him up to the arms
of justice. A hook is then baited and cast into the
river or lake. Next day the guilty brother or one
of his family is dragged ashore, formally tried, sen-
tenced to death, and executed. The claims of justice
being thus satisfied, the dead animal is lamented
and buried like a kinsman ; a mound is raised over
his grave and a stone marks the place of his head.[1]

Amongst the Tshi-speaking tribes of the Gold
Coast in West Africa the Horse-mackerel family
traces its descent from a real horse-mackerel whom
an ancestor of theirs once took to wife. She lived
with him happily in human shape on shore till one
day a second wife, whom the man had married,
cruelly taunted her with being nothing but a fish.
That hurt her so much that, bidding her husband
farewell, she returned to her old home in the sea,
with her youngest child in her arms, and never
came back again. But ever since the Horse-
mackerel people have refrained from eating horse-
mackerels, because the lost wife and mother was a
fish of that sort.[2] Some of the Land Dyaks of

[1] Father Abinal, " Croyances
fabuleuses des Malgaches ", Les
Missions Catholiques, xii. (1880),
p. 527 ; A. van Gennep, Tabou
et Totémisme à Madagascar, pp.

281 sq.
[2] A. B. Ellis, The Tshi-speaking Peoples of the Gold Coast of
West Africa (London, 1887), pp.
208-211. A similar tale is told

Borneo tell a similar tale to explain a similar custom. "There is a fish which is taken in their rivers called a *puttin*, which they would on no account touch, under the idea that if they did they would be eating their relations. The tradition respecting it is, that a solitary old man went out fishing and caught a *puttin*, which he dragged out of the water and laid down in his boat. On turning round, he found it had changed into a very pretty little girl. Conceiving the idea she would make, what he had long wished for, a charming wife for his son, he took her home and educated her until she was fit to be married. She consented to be the son's wife, cautioning her husband to use her well. Some time after their marriage, however, being out of temper, he struck her, when she screamed, and rushed away into the water ; but not without leaving behind her a beautiful daughter, who became afterwards the mother of the race." [1]

Members of a clan in Mandailing, on the west coast of Sumatra, assert that they are descended from a tiger, and at the present day, when a tiger is shot, the women of the clan are bound to offer

by another Fish family who abstain from eating the fish (*appei*) from which they take their name (A. B. Ellis, *op. cit.* pp. 211 *sq.*).

[1] The Lord Bishop of Labuan, " On the Wild Tribes of the North-West Coast of Borneo ", *Transactions of the Ethnological Society of London*, New Series, ii. (London, 1863), pp. 26 *sq.* Such stories conform to a well-known type which may be called the Swan-Maiden type of story, or Beauty and the Beast, or Cupid and Psyche. The occurrence of stories of this type among totemic peoples, such as the Tshi-speaking negroes of the Gold Coast, who tell them to explain their totemic taboos, suggests that all such tales may have originated in totemism. I shall deal with this question elsewhere.

betel to the dead beast.   When members of this clan come upon the tracks of a tiger, they must, as a mark of homage, enclose them with three little sticks.   Further, it is believed that the tiger will not attack or lacerate his kinsmen, the members of the clan.[1] The Battas of Central Sumatra are divided into a number of clans which have for their totems white buffaloes, goats, wild turtle-doves, dogs, cats, apes, tigers, and so forth ; and one of the explanations which they give of their totems is that these creatures were their ancestors, and that their own souls after death can transmigrate into che animals.[2] In Amboyna and the neighbouring islands the inhabitants of some villages aver that they are descended from trees, such as the *Capellenia moluccana*, which had been fertilized by the *Pandion Haliaetus*. Others claim to be sprung from pigs, octopuses, crocodiles, sharks, and eels.   People will not burn the wood of the trees from which they trace their descent, nor eat the flesh of the animals which they regard as their ancestors.   Sicknesses of all sorts are believed to result from disregarding these taboos.[3] Similarly in Ceram persons who think

[1] H. Ris, " De Onderafdeeling Klein Mandailing Oeloe en Pahantan en hare Bevolking met uitzondering van de Oelos ", *Bijdragen tot de Taal- Land- en Volkenkunde van Nederlandsch-Indië*, xlvi. (1896), p. 473.

[2] J. B. Neumann, " Het Pane en Bila-stroomgebied op het eiland Sumatra ", *Tijdscrift van het Nederlandsch Aardrijkskundig Genootschap*, Tweede Serie, iii. Afdeeling, Meer uitgebreide Artikelen, No. 2 (Amsterdam, 1886), pp. 311 *sq.* ; *id. ib.*, Tweede Serie, iv. Afdeeling, Meer uitgebreide Artikelen, No. 1 (Amsterdam, 1887), pp. 8 *sq.*

[3] J. G. F. Riedel, *De sluik- en kroesharige rassen tusschen Selebes en Papua* (The Hague, 1886), pp. 32, 61 ; G. W. W. C. Baron van Hoëvell, *Ambon en meer bepaaldelijk de Oeliasers* (Dordrecht, 1875), p. 152.

they are descended from crocodiles, serpents, igu-
anas, and sharks will not eat the flesh of these
animals.[1] Many other peoples of the Molucca
Islands entertain similar beliefs and observe similar
taboos.[2] Again, in Ponape, one of the Caroline
Islands, " the different families suppose themselves
to stand in a certain relation to animals, and especially to fishes, and believe in their descent from them.
They actually name these animals ' mothers '; the
creatures are sacred to the family and may not be
injured. Great dances, accompanied with the offer-
ing of prayers, are performed in their honour. Any
person who killed such an animal would expose
himself to contempt and punishment, certainly also
to the vengeance of the insulted deity." Blindness
is commonly supposed to be the consequence of such
a sacrilege.[3]

Some of the aborigines of Western Australia
believe that their ancestors were swans, ducks, or
various other species of water-fowl before they were
transformed into men.[4] The Dieri tribe of Central
Australia, who are divided into totemic clans, explain their origin by the following legend. They
say that in the beginning the earth opened in the
midst of Perigundi Lake, and the totems (*murdus*
or *madas*) came trooping out one after the other.

[1] J. G. F. Riedel, *op. cit.* p.
122.

[2] J. G. F. Riedel, *De sluik- en
kroesharige rassen tusschen Selebes en Papua* (The Hague, 1886),
pp. 253, 334, 341, 348, 412, 414,
432.

[3] Dr. Hahl, " Mitteilungen

über Sitten und rechtliche Ver-
hältnisse auf Ponape ", *Ethno-
logisches Notizblatt*, vol. ii. Heft
2 (Berlin, 1901), p. 10.

[4] Captain G. Grey, *A Voca-
bulary of the Dialects of South
Western Australia*, Second Edition (London, 1840), pp. 29, 37,
61, 63, 66, 71.

Out came the crow, and the shell parakeet, and the emu, and all the rest. Being as yet imperfectly formed and without members or organs of sense, they laid themselves down on the sandhills which surrounded the lake then just as they do now. It was a bright day and the totems lay basking in the sunshine, till at last, refreshed and invigorated by it, they stood up as human beings and dispersed in all directions. That is why people of the same totem are now scattered all over the country. You may still see the island in the lake out of which the totems came trooping long ago.[1] Another Dieri legend relates how Paralina, one of the *Mura-Muras* or mythical predecessors of the Dieri, perfected mankind. He was out hunting kangaroos, when he saw four incomplete beings cowering together. So he went up to them, smoothed their bodies, stretched out their limbs, slit up their fingers and toes, formed their mouths, noses, and eyes, stuck ears on them, and blew into their ears in order that they might hear. Having perfected their organs and so produced mankind out of these rudimentary beings, he went about making men everywhere.[2] Yet another Dieri tradition sets forth how the *Mura-Mura* produced the race of man out of a species of small black lizards, which may still be met with under dry bark. To do this he divided the feet of the lizards into fingers and toes, and applying his forefinger to the middle of their faces, created a nose ; likewise he gave them human eyes,

[1] A. W. Howitt, *Native Tribes of South-East Australia* (London, 1904), pp. 476, 779 *sq.*

[2] A. W. Howitt, *op. cit.* pp. 476, 780 *sq.*

mouths, and ears. He next set one of them upright, but it fell down again because of its tail ; so
he cut off its tail and the lizard then walked on its
hind legs. That is the origin of mankind.[1]

The Arunta tribe of Central Australia similarly
tell how in the beginning mankind was developed
out of various rudimentary forms of animal life.
They say that in those days two beings called *Ungambikula*, that is, " out of nothing ", or " self-
existing ", dwelt in the western sky. From their
lofty abode they could see, far away to the east, a
number of *inapertwa* creatures, that is, rudimentary
human beings or incomplete men, whom it was their
mission to make into real men and women. For at
that time there were no real men and women ; the
rudimentary creatures (*inapertwa*) were of various
shapes and dwelt in groups along the shore of the
salt water which covered the country. These embryos, as we may call them, had no distinct limbs
or organs of sight, hearing, and smell ; they did not
eat food, and they presented the appearance of
human beings all doubled up into a rounded mass,
in which only the outline of the different parts of the
body could be vaguely perceived. Coming down
from their home in the western sky, armed with
great stone knives, the *Ungambikula* took hold of
the embryos, one after the other. First of all they

[1] S. Gason, " The Manners
and Customs of the Dieyerie
Tribe of Australian Aborigines ",
Native Tribes of South Australia
(Adelaide, 1879), p. 260. This
writer fell into the mistake of re-
garding the *Mura-Mura* (*Moora-*
moora) as a Good Spirit instead
of as one of the mythical but more
or less human predecessors of
the Dieri in the country. See
A. W. Howitt, *Native Tribes of
South-East Australia*, pp. 475
sqq.

released the arms from the bodies, then, making four clefts at the end of each arm, they fashioned hands and fingers ; afterwards legs, feet, and toes were added in the same way. The figure could now stand ; a nose was then moulded and the nostrils bored with the fingers. A cut with the knife made the mouth, which was pulled open several times to render it flexible. A slit on each side of the face separated the upper and lower eyelids, disclosing the eyes, which already existed behind them ; and a few strokes more completed the body. Thus out of the rudimentary creatures were formed men and women. These rudimentary creatures or embryos, we are told, " were in reality stages in the transformation of various animals and plants into human beings, and thus they were naturally, when made into human beings, intimately associated with the particular animal or plant, as the case may be, of which they were the transformations—in other words, each individual of necessity belonged to a totem, the name of which was of course that of the animal or plant of which he or she was a transformation ". However, it is not said that all the totemic clans of the Arunta were thus developed ; no such tradition, for example, is told to explain the origin of the important Witchetty Grub clan. The clans which are positively known, or at least said, to have originated out of embryos in the way described are the Plum Tree, the Grass Seed, the Large Lizard, the Small Lizard, the Alexandra Parakeet, and the Small Rat clans. When the *Ungambikula* had thus fashioned people of these totems, they circumcised them all, except the Plum Tree men, by means of a fire-stick.   After that, having done the work of creation or evolution, the *Ungambikula* turned themselves into little lizards which bear a name meaning " snappers-up of flies ".[1]

This Arunta tradition of the origin of man, as Messrs. Spencer and Gillen, who have recorded it, justly observe, " is of considerable interest ; it is in the first place evidently a crude attempt to describe the origin of human beings out of non-human creatures who were of various forms ; some of them were representatives of animals, others of plants, but in all cases they are to be regarded as intermediate stages in the transition of an animal or plant ancestor into a human individual who bore its name as that of his or her totem ".[2]   In a sense these speculations of the Arunta on their own origin may be said to combine the theory of creation with the theory of evolution ; for while they represent men as developed out of much simpler forms of life, they at the same time assume that this development was effected by the agency of two powerful beings, whom so far we may call creators.   It is well known that at a far higher stage of culture a crude form of the evolutionary hypothesis was propounded by the Greek philosopher Empedocles.   He imagined that shapeless lumps of earth and water, thrown up by the subterranean fires, developed into monstrous animals, bulls with the heads of men, men with the heads of bulls, and so forth ; till at last, these hybrid

[1] Baldwin Spencer and F. J. Gillen, *Native Tribes of Central Australia* (London, 1899), pp. 388 *sq.* ; compare *id.*, *Northern Tribes of Central Australia* (London, 1904), p. 150.

[2] Baldwin Spencer and F. J. Gillen, *Native Tribes of Central Australia*, pp. 391 *sq.*

forms being gradually eliminated, the various existing species of animals and men were evolved.[1]   The
theory of the civilized Greek of Sicily may be set
beside the similar theory of the savage Arunta of
Central Australia.   Both represent gropings of the
human mind in the dark abyss of the past ; both
were in a measure grotesque anticipations of the
modern theory of evolution.

In this essay I have made no attempt to illustrate all
the many various and divergent views which primitive
man has taken of his own origin.   I have confined
myself to collecting examples of two radically different views, which may be distinguished as the theory
of creation and the theory of evolution.   According
to the one, man was fashioned in his existing shape
by a god or other powerful being : according to
the other he was evolved by a natural process out
of lower forms of animal life.   Roughly speaking,
these two theories still divide the civilized world
between them.   The partisans of each can appeal
in support of their view to a large consensus of
opinion ; and if truth were to be decided by weigh-
ing the one consensus against the other, with *Genesis*
in the one scale and *The Origin of Species* in the
other, it might perhaps be found, when the scales
were finally trimmed, that the balance hung very
even between creation and evolution.

[1] E. Zeller, *Die Philosophie der
Griechen*, i.[4] (Leipsic, 1876), pp.
718 *sq.* ; H. Ritter et L. Preller,
*Historia Philosophiae Graecae et
Romanae ex fontium locis con-*
texta [5], pp. 102 *sq.* ; H. Diels,
Die Fragmente der Vorsokra-
tiker [3], i. (Berlin, 1906), pp. 190
sqq.   Compare Lucretius, *De
rerum natura*, v. 837 *sqq.*

MEDIAEVAL LATIN FABULISTS

(From *The Academy*, 8th November 1884, No. 653,
pp. 300, 301)

II

MEDIAEVAL LATIN FABULISTS

THE fables of Phaedrus seem to have been but little read in antiquity, if we may judge from the fact that their author is only mentioned by Martial and Avianus, while the imitations of his works are confined to a few by the former poet, and a stray one by Prudentius. But if the influence of Phaedrus was small in antiquity, it was correspondingly great in the Middle Ages. True, his name was forgotten, and his works in their original shape lost ; but the substance of his fables was preserved in prose versions, which became, in their turn, the source of more or less divergent collections of fables in Latin prose and verse, as well as in Old French, Old English, and Low German.

M. Hervieux has done good service by collecting and publishing the texts of all the Latin imitations of Phaedrus which have survived from the Middle Ages.[1] In pursuit of his plan he has visited most of the public libraries of Europe, and has himself copied, or had copied by others, all the collections of Latin fables to be found. Some of these

---

[1] *Les Fabulistes Latins,* depuis le siècle d'Auguste jusqu'à la fin du moyen âge. Par Léopold Hervieux. In 2 vols. (Paris : Firmin-Didot).

collections are now published for the first time ; in
the case of others which have been published before,
M. Hervieux has collated fresh manuscripts. Thus
we have now, for the first time, an edition of the
important collection of Latin prose fables contained
in the Weissenburg (now Wolfenbüttel) MS. As
against Oesterley, who lightly assumed that this
collection as well as that known as the Anonymous
of Nilant, were mere extracts from the celebrated
collection which bears the name of *Romulus*, M.
Hervieux has proved by comparison of the texts
that the three collections are independent, and that
the Anonymous of Nilant is even older than
Romulus, that in fact it is the oldest known para-
phrase of Phaedrus, to which it bears so close a
resemblance (preserving whole verses intact) that
it must have been made directly from the text of
Phaedrus. With regard to the so-called *Romulus*,
M. Hervieux shows what had been suspected before,
that he is the mere fiction of a copyist, who thought
to give fresh dignity and interest to an old collection
of fables by prefixing to them a preface in which a
certain Romulus, addressing his son Tyberinus, pro-
fesses to have translated them directly from the
Greek. But this lying scribe was a fool as well as a
knave, for in calmly transcribing the preface (ad-
dressed to one Rufus) of the previous collection, he
has left us the proof of his falsehood. Still, his
puppet of a Romulus long escaped detection. He
passed for a Roman emperor in the Middle Ages,
and he still survives, though shorn of his imperial
dignity, in the pages of the *Biographie Universelle*.
In editing the text of *Romulus*, M. Hervieux has

followed the Munich MS. 753, which he collated
personally. This is admittedly the most recent of
the MSS. of *Romulus*, being written by Crinitus, of
Florence, in 1495 ; but as the older MSS.—the
Codex Divionensis (now lost, but the copy made by
Guden in 1660–1663 is extant in the Wolfenbüttel
library), and the Codex Burneianus (in the British
Museum)—had been already collated and edited,
M. Hervieux did well in breaking new ground, for
he has thus proved that, notwithstanding the many
collections derived from *Romulus*, the primitive text
survived down to the Renaissance. Another MS.
of *Romulus*, collated by M. Hervieux, that of Corpus
Christi College, Oxford, belongs to the fourteenth
century, and is thus intermediate between the
Munich MS. on the one side and the older Burneianus (tenth century) and Divionensis (twelfth
century) on the other. Amongst the fables in verse
to which *Romulus* gave rise there is one in Latin
elegiacs which enjoyed a wide popularity in the
Middle Ages. The authorship of this collection has
long been a matter of discussion ; since the edition
of Névelet in 1610 it has usually been known as the
Anonymous of Névelet. M. Hervieux believes that
he has succeeded in identifying the author with
Walther of England, chaplain to Henry II., and
afterwards Archbishop of Palermo. He relies on a
gloss in a MS.[1] (Lat. 303) in the Imperial library at

[1] The gloss runs thus : " Ti-
tulus ei talis est : *Incipit Esopus*,
quod non fuit nomen composi-
toris sed Waltherus. Ut autem
eius liber honestius reciperetur,
intitulavit eum hoc nomine ".
The glosser proceeds to suggest
that Æsop (Esopus) is either
the name of a " nobilis quidam ",
or is simply the herb hyssop (!),
and that Walther gave his book
this name because, like the hyssop,
it was good for a variety of
purposes !

Vienna, and on another gloss in the edition printed at Lyons in 1480 (" Galterus Anglicus fecit hunc librum sub nomine Esopi "). Without sharing M. Hervieux's absolute confidence in the certainty of his discovery, we may admit that he has made out a case which has no inherent improbability, and agrees with the date of the oldest MS. (thirteenth century), and we may note as a confirmatory circumstance the special popularity which these verse fables enjoyed in Italy, as attested by the numerous editions and translations of them published in that country—a popularity partly explicable on the hypothesis that the author was Archbishop of Palermo.

If M. Hervieux's theory is true, it adds another to the not inconsiderable list of collections of fables made by Englishmen or in England during the Middle Ages. Such are the collections of the two monks—Odo of Sherrington and Alexander Neckam. The former, about A.D. 1200, composed a large number of prose fables, of which only a part can be traced to *Romulus*. His fables have a strong mediaeval and ecclesiastical flavour, the devil is frequently introduced to point the moral, and the author does not spare the faults of his clerical brethren. M. Hervieux maintains, against Voigt, that the fables of Odo are not to be reduced to sixty, and he is the first to publish them in their entirety. Alexander Neckam, Abbot of the Augustinian monastery at Exeter in 1215, among numerous other works, was the author of forty-two fables in Latin elegiacs, most of them based on *Romulus*. Though translated into French verse in the thirteenth century, they never had the same vogue as those of

Walther. But of the mediaeval fables derived
directly from Phaedrus, the most celebrated, perhaps, are those in Old-French verse by Marie de
France, who resided in England in the thirteenth
century. She wrote her fables, she tells us, " for
the love of Count William " :

> Pur amur le cumte Willaume
> Le plus vaillant de cest royaume.

Who this Count William may have been is a matter
of dispute. M. Hervieux, agreeing with the Abbé
de la Rue, decides in favour of William Long-Sword,
son of Henry II. and the fair Rosamond, created
Earl of Salisbury by Cœur-de-Lion. The version
of Marie was made, as she tells us, from an English
translation, the work of an English king, whose
name appears in various forms in the MSS. Most
of these forms seem to be corruptions of Alfred ;
but, on the strength of two MSS., M. Hervieux
identifies the royal translator with Henry I. Beau-
Clerc. No other trace of this translation exists ;
but we possess twenty-two Latin fables which
appear to be a portion of that version of *Romulus*
from which the English translation was made. M.
Hervieux has shed fresh light on this Latin original by publishing 136 fables, extracted from MSS.
of Trèves, Göttingen, Brussels, and the British
Museum, which he believes to have been derived
from the same version of *Romulus* as that from
which the English translation referred to by Marie
was made. Of these 136 fables, 95 are now published for the first time.

A conclusion forced upon us by the mediaeval

prose versions of Phaedrus is that our present copies
of Phaedrus, even with the addition of the " new "
fables preserved in the MS. of Perotti, are far from
complete.   Of the one hundred distinct fables preserved in the three oldest of these versions (Anonymous of Nilant, Weissenberg collection, *Romulus*),
forty-six have no counterpart in our Phaedrus.   But
when we consider the close resemblance which those
fables whose original is Phaedrus bear to that
original, it seems a reasonable inference that the
remaining fables of the same collections are equally
close copies of lost fables of Phaedrus.   As a matter
of fact the discovery of the " new " fables of
Phaedrus at once furnished the original of eight of
the fables of *Romulus*, of which the origin had been
previously unknown.   If we had a complete Phaedrus, we should probably find in it the originals of all
the fables contained in the three prose collections in
question.   This inference is justly drawn by M.
Hervieux, who is as judicious as he is learned.   His
present work, the first instalment of a larger one,
includes Phaedrus and his Latin imitators, direct
and indirect, down to the close of the Middle Ages.
The first of these two large and handsome volumes
is devoted to a discussion of the lives and works of
Phaedrus and his imitators and the relations which
these bear to each other, and includes an elaborate
account of the editions and MSS. of their works.
In the list of editions it is surprising to see that M.
Hervieux has overlooked the important edition of
Phaedrus by Lucian Müller, Teubner, 1877.   The
notices of his own researches and of the lives of some
of the scholars whom he has occasion to mention

add much to the interest of M. Hervieux's well-written book. The second volume contains the texts of the authors, from Phaedrus down to Neckam. It is M. Hervieux's intention to treat the other Latin fabulists in the same way, beginning with Avianus. We sincerely trust that the learned editor will live to complete the important work which he has thus far so admirably executed.

GIBBON AT LAUSANNE

(Extrait des *Mélanges Glotz*, Presse Universitaire, Paris, tome I, p. 381)

III

GIBBON AT LAUSANNE

In recent times there has come into vogue a fashion
of writing history on a large scale by confederate
bands of scholars, each of whom brings to the task a
special knowledge of a particular period or a particular aspect of the subject to be treated. Conspicuous examples of this method of composing
history, which we may call the collective or co-
operative method, are afforded by Lavisse's well-
known history of France and the Cambridge his-
tories of antiquity, the Middle Ages, and modern
times. It is on this plan that Professor Glotz has
chosen to construct the great history of the world
which is now appearing under his general editorship, and to which he is himself contributing the old,
but ever fresh and fascinating, story of ancient
Greece from the earliest times down to the Roman
conquest. The plan has much to recommend it.
With the ever lengthening span of human existence
on earth and the ever accumulating mass of docu-
mentary evidence, which the marvellous inventions
of modern science tend constantly to multiply to a
degree and in directions of which former generations
did not even dream, so that our remote posterity
will be able not only to read of us but to see and hear

47

us acting and speaking as in life, it becomes ever less and less possible for any individual, within the short compass of a single lifetime, to embrace the prodigious number of facts on record and to digest them into a history. Accordingly scholars who propose to deal with long periods of human history tend more and more to resort to that division of labour which has long proved so fruitful in science, and without which, indeed, the enormous advances of scientific discovery in our own and our fathers' time would have been wholly impossible. A history thus composed by the joint efforts of several or many scholars is likely to attain a higher degree both of fullness and of accuracy than one composed by the unassisted labour of a single scholar, however learned and able he may be ; and as the proper aim of history is to give a full and accurate account of the past, we may conclude that it will probably best achieve its object when it is constructed on the collective or co-operative plan to which Professor Glotz has rightly given the preference in the great historical work for which he stands sponsor.

But while the new collective or co-operative method of historical composition possesses these obvious and substantial advantages, something may still be urged in favour of the old plan of leaving the task of composing history, even a long history, to the spontaneous initiative and unaided labours of a single writer. For that plan permits of a unity and harmony of conception and execution such as are hardly compatible with the diversity of authorship involved in the collective method. It was the plan universally followed in antiquity, and we cannot

unreservedly condemn its prevalence of old when
we remember that we are indebted to it for the sil-
very accents of Herodotus, the crystalline prose of
Xenophon, the tragic grandeur of Thucydides and
Tacitus, and the limpid stream of Livy's eloquence.
In modern times the example of these old masters
has been followed by not a few of the great historians
of Italy and France, of Germany and England,
whose works are classical.

Of these great historians, the ornaments of their
country and of mankind, there is one whom it seems
particularly fitting to recall on this occasion and at
this place, Lausanne, where I am writing. For it
was at Lausanne that Gibbon wrote the latter half
of his *History of the Decline and Fall of the Roman
Empire*, thereby completing the last arches of that
golden bridge along which he led his enchanted
readers from ancient to modern times. The solidity
and beauty of the architecture of the bridge will
strike us as all the more wonderful when we remember the wretched nature of the materials of
which it was built. The history of the Decline and
Fall begins very aptly at the precise moment when
the great literature of antiquity expired, and it ends
when the great literature of modern Europe was still
unborn ; the period which it covers was the night
of the Middle Ages, between the melancholy sunset
of the old world and the splendid dawn of the new.
On that night, it is true, Dante had risen like the
Morning Star of the day that was about to break ;
but the long hours of darkness had been illumined
by not a single contemporary historian of genius,
hardly even by one of the second rank, if we except

Procopius, whose scandalous chronicle sheds a lurid light on Byzantium in the time of Justinian, like the last angry flush of sunset in a stormy sky over a doomed city. All the more, therefore, must we marvel at the wizardry of Gibbon, who by his alchemic touch could turn the lead and dross of the dreary Byzantine annals into the liquid gold of his stately periods. It would be no matter for wonder if some modern historian were to give to the world as masterly and eloquent a history of ancient Greece; the wonder rather is that no one has yet done so, though the materials for such a work exist in profusion in the noble literature which the destroying hand of Time has yet spared to a late posterity. Nothing perhaps enables us to gauge better the height and depth of the Greek genius than a comparison of its literature with the uses which modern writers have made of it in their attempts to set forth the history of Greece in its prime. It was reserved for an Englishman to record the decline and fall of Greek civilization in its last stronghold at Byzantium with a fidelity, an insight, an amplitude of view, and an eloquence worthy to rank with the literary masterpieces of Grecian antiquity.

The historian has himself commemorated the moment both of the first conception of his immortal work and of the last stroke of the pen that he put to it. He conceived the plan on his first, and indeed his last, visit to Rome, on the 15th of October 1764, while he sat among the ruins of the Capitol, listening to the bare-footed friars singing vespers in the temple of Jupiter. The time, the place, the music, all conspired to suggest the great idea. The

sunset light falling on the ruins and lingering in a
rosy glow on the crests of the distant Appenines,
while the shadows of night crept up their lower
slopes, and the solemn evening hymn, vibrating on
the air, composed the mind of the listener to pensive
musings, formed a fitting scene and accompaniment
for the conception of a work that was to tell of the
passing away of an old world and an outworn faith
and the coming of a new world and a new religion.

The great history was finished at Lausanne between the hours of eleven and twelve of a summer
night, the 27th of June 1787.   When he had written
the last line of the last page in a summer-house in his
garden, the historian laid down his pen and took
several turns in a covered walk of acacias, which
commanded a prospect of the country, the lake, and
the mountains.   The air was temperate, the sky
was serene, the silver orb of the moon was mirrored
in the shimmering waters of the lake, and all nature
was silent.   As he paced to and fro in the solitude
and stillness of the summer night, the author sur-
rendered himself for a time to the emotions which
the occasion was naturally fitted to evoke.   But the
first ebullition of joy at the completion of his life-
work and perhaps the establishment of his fame
soon subsided and gave way to a calmer and graver
mood : he reflected, with a sober melancholy, that
he had bidden an everlasting farewell to an old and
agreeable companion, and that whatever the future
fate of his *History* might be, the life of the historian
must be short and precarious.   In fact, he survived
the triumph of that summer night for about seven
years, which he spent in contented retirement for

the most part at Lausanne, without adding materially to his reputation by his writings, if we except, as indeed we are bound to do, his *Autobiography*, which must ever rank with the best models of its kind for the engaging candour of its narrative and the polished elegance of its style. Yet though he passed the serene evening of his life in his beloved Swiss retreat, he did not end his days there. He died, appropriately enough, in his native England, and his dust rests in English earth, though not among his peers, the illustrious dead in Westminster Abbey. But he needed no funeral honours, no monument of brass or marble to his fame : in his great *History* he has built himself a monument which is numbered among the glories of modern literature and can only perish with the English tongue. And Lausanne, the home of his youth, the scene of his most mature labours, and the chosen haven of his declining years, will always be associated with his memory and share the reflected lustre of his renown.

LAUSANNE, *October* 1931.

BALDWIN SPENCER AS
ANTHROPOLOGIST

IV

BALDWIN SPENCER AS ANTHROPO-LOGIST

THE early life of Spencer may be said to have been a fortunate, though necessarily undesigned, preparation for the great work which he accomplished in the maturity of his powers. His training in biology and zoology familiarized him with the conception of physical evolution in the animal and human species, and at Oxford the teaching of Tylor, the true founder of anthropology in England, initiated him in the elements of mental and social evolution in the history of man. Thus, when the happy circumstance of a call to Melbourne led Spencer to settle in Australia, he was well prepared to grasp the significance of the primitive, or rather archaic, forms of plant, animal, and human life, which the immemorial seclusion of that continent from the rest of the world has preserved as in a museum to satisfy the curiosity of later ages concerning the development of life on our planet. In his new home Spencer's attention was naturally drawn at first to those early forms of animal life which it was his special duty, as Professor of Zoology at Melbourne University, to investigate. But, later on, his fortunate attachment to the Horn Expedition led him to make the acquaintance of the Arunta, the great aboriginal tribe in the very heart of Australia, who, dwelling in the most isolated region of the most isolated continent, have survived to our time as if on purpose to hold up to us a mirror of the life of man as it was in ages long before the dawn of history. To have discovered the picture, or rather the long series of pictures, in the mirror and revealed it to science is the outstanding achievement of Spencer and must ensure for him, for all time to come, a foremost place among the pioneers of anthropology. He had, indeed, an able and enthusiastic colleague in the person of his friend F. J. Gillen, who, as Protector of the Aborigines, had lived among the Arunta and had amassed a considerable body of information concerning them before Spencer visited the tribe for the first time in 1894 ; but it is probably doing no injustice to the memory of the genial Irishman to suppose that, like many men in similar contact with primitive peoples, he would have passed away without leaving any record of his priceless knowledge if it had not been for the inspiration and direction of Spencer.   Henceforth the two men devoted all the leisure which their professional duties allowed them to deepening and widening their acquaintance with the aboriginal tribes spread over an immense area of Australia, from the dreary wilderness of Lake Eyre in the south to the shores of the Gulf of Carpentaria on the north.   After Gillen's death Spencer still further extended the range of his researches by studying the tribes of North-West Australia in the neighbourhood of Port Darwin, including the interesting and little-known tribes of

Bathurst and Melville Islands. But the tribe which he and Gillen knew best was the Arunta ; it remained the central point of their studies and supplied in a sense the standard by which they judged the rest. The last work but one which Spencer published was a monograph on the Arunta, which embodied all the information given by him and Gillen jointly on this particular tribe in *The Native Tribes of Central Australia*, but enlarged by the addition of fresh and valuable materials which Spencer alone had collected from the surviving old men of the tribe in the course of investigations which he undertook in the latter years of his life for the purpose of correcting or corroborating his former accounts on doubtful matters. The result of these, his latest Australian researches, was to confirm his original information on all essential points.

The general outcome of Spencer's work on the aborigines of Australia, of whom in his long and laborious researches he had acquired a more extensive and exact knowledge than any man before him had acquired or than any man after him can hope to acquire of this dying race, was to place on record a full, detailed, and exact description of a people living in the Stone Age, without metals, without clothes, without houses, without domestic animals (except dogs), and not only without agriculture but without even the conception that seeds will grow and multiply if you plant them in the ground. For subsistence these folk depended entirely on the flesh of the animals which the men killed, and on the vegetable food which the women gathered from the trees and plants, supplemented by the seeds and roots which they grubbed up with their digging-sticks, but which it never occurred to them to plant again in the ground for the sake of ensuring, in a subsequent crop, a manifold return for the temporary sacrifice of the food which they had committed to the earth. As for sheep and cattle, they were necessarily destitute of them for the sufficient reason that no such creatures existed in Australia until they were imported from Europe. Thus the material condition of these savages was the simplest and lowest consistent with the existence of human life on earth.

But if their material life was of the simplest possible kind, it was by no means so with their social and even intellectual life. For they had created a social system which, in regard to the relation of the sexes, was far more complicated and strict than any recorded in the history of civilized nations in any part of the world. And though their capacity to count did not exceed the first few digits, they had evolved an elaborate system of mythology based on the belief in the survival of human souls after death and their subsequent rebirth in an endless succession of human generations. Their fertile imagination peopled the wilderness—the rugged rocks, the desolate hills, the solitary trees, the lonely tarns—with the spirits of the dead awaiting reincarnation and watching for women passing by in order to dart into them and be born again into the world. For, ignorant of the part played by the male in the reproduction of the species, they firmly believed that conception was thus effected by the entrance of a spirit into the mother's womb, and that the place where she first felt the new burden was the spot where, at the same moment, the soul of the infant had entered into her.   Strange as it may seem to us, this ignorance of physiological paternity must at one time have been universally prevalent among mankind, and though most savages are now aware of the part played by the father in the begetting of children, the childish ignorance on the subject still survives as an isolated phenomenon in some parts of the world, as in the Trobriand Islands, the natives of which nevertheless stand at a much higher level of culture than the Australian aborigines, since they subsist mainly by agriculture, or rather horticulture, live in settled dwellings, and engage in seafaring and commerce.   But Spencer and Gillen were the first to record this more than Arcadian simplicity in regard to the birth of children among existing savages, and it is not the least remarkable of their discoveries for the light it throws on the mental condition of primeval man.   The observations made by them in this respect among the natives of Central Australia were soon afterwards independently confirmed, or rather extended, for the aborigines of Queensland by the Rev. Dr. Frodsham, Bishop of that diocese.   The scepticism with which the evidence of first-rate observers on this point has been received by some critics is only one proof more of the utter incapacity of many civilized men to place themselves at the point of view of uncivilized humanity.

The same curious belief as to the birth of children furnishes the clue to the otherwise apparently inexplicable totemic system of the Central Australian aborigines ; for, like savages in many parts of the world, they had a system of totemism, which indeed formed, we may almost say, the very core of their social and intellectual life. But unlike totems elsewhere, which are usually inherited by children from their father or their mother, the totems of the Central Australian aborigines are not derived from their parents at all but are determined by the spot where the mother first felt her womb quickened, because there, they believe, the spirit of the infant entered into her from the nearest natural object, whether stone or tree or what not, in which the congregated spirits of one particular totem (for example, a kangaroo or an opossum) had been waiting to pounce out on women and be born of them again into the world. Such natural objects, each haunted by spirits of a particular totem, are known as local totem centres ; and if a woman first feels the child stirring in her womb near one of them which is haunted, for instance, by spirits that had the kangaroo for their totem, then her child, when it is born, will also have the kangaroo for its totem ; and so on with all the rest.

And their unquestioning faith in the survival of the spirits of the dead has affected the life of the tribes in another way ; it has endowed them with a drama. For a considerable part of their abundant leisure is devoted to representing dramatically the legendary doings of their ancestors, who are believed to have roamed about the country creating all the more conspicuous landmarks, whether rocks or trees or pools, which vary the otherwise monotonous and dreary expanse of the Central Australian wilder-

ness ; and although, so far as I remember, the
authors do not affirm it, we may perhaps conjecture
that the spirits of the dead ancestors, lurking unseen
in the rocks or trees, are believed to be gratified by
the sight of these commemorative services. Thus
far, therefore, the example of these primitive Australian dramas may be thought to confirm by ana-
logy the theory of the late Sir William Ridgeway,
that Greek tragedy originated in the commemora-
tion and propitiation of the dead.

But the dramas of the Central Australian aborigines are by no means all simply commemorative.
A very important class of them is purely magical,
being designed to maintain and multiply by magic
the natural sources of subsistence, whether vegetable
or animal, whether solid or liquid, on which the
very existence of the community is dependent. It
would, therefore, be difficult to exaggerate the importance which the natives attach to the proper per-
formance of these magical rites ; it is for them a
matter of life and death. The essence of the rites
consists in mimicking the object which the performers desire to produce ; for the principle of magic
on which they proceed is that of sympathy or imita-
tion ; the ceremony must resemble the effect which
it is meant to bring about. If the intention, for
example, is to produce a supply of edible insects, the
performers imitate the shape and movements of the
creature ; if they desire to secure a supply of water,
they imitate the fall of rain; and so on with the other
departments of nature which are to be magically
kept in working order.

Now this system of satisfying all the material

wants of life by means of magic is ingeniously dove-
tailed by these savages into their totemic system,
or rather perhaps forms an integral part of it.   For,
roughly speaking, they have subdivided the whole
of nature into totems, and have distributed the various departments of nature, as totems, among the
totemic clans, charging each clan with the duty of
maintaining its own particular department, that is,
its totem (it may be a species of plants or animals, or
water, or the sun, or what not), for the public good
by means of imitative magic.   Thus the whole tribe
forms, as it were, a single great co-operative society,
working together, by a system of co-ordinated activities, for the maintenance of nature in the interest
of man ; the aim and intention are thoroughly practical, and to all appearance the results are entirely
satisfactory.   For undoubtedly nature continues to
pursue its regular course in Central Australia : edible
plants still grow and edible animals still multiply ; the
sun still shines, and rain still falls, if only you wait
long enough for it.   What better proof could the Australian native desire of the efficacy of his magic ?

   This revelation of totemism as, in one of its
aspects, an industrial system of co-operative magic
for the supply of human wants is one of the great
discoveries of Spencer and Gillen.   No such system,
at once social, industrial, and magical, so complete
in its organization and so far-reaching in its aims,
has yet been recorded in any other part of the
world, though what may be isolated fragments of
such a system have here and there been noted in the
shape of magical rites for the maintenance or multiplication of totems.

One particular feature of the Australian magical rites for the multiplication of totems is deserving of special notice. In general these Central Australians observe the common rule of totemism which forbids a man to kill and eat his totemic animal, or to gather and eat his totemic plant. But to this rule the savages in question make a very remarkable exception ; before a man performs a magical ceremony for the multiplication of his totem, he is obliged to kill and eat a small portion of it, if it is an animal, or to gather and eat a little of it, if it is a plant. Should he not thus partake of his totemic animal or plant, it is believed that his magic would be ineffectual to produce a supply of it for the benefit of those members of the tribe who do not belong to his totemic clan and are therefore free to partake of his totemic animal or plant. Apparently, though we are not told so expressly, the notion is that by eating of the totemic animal or plant a man identifies himself with his totem and so acquires the power of multiplying it. Thus the eating of the totem is in a sense a totemic sacrament, such as the genius of William Robertson Smith divined the existence of long before any clear case of it had been discovered in practice.

Such are in brief outline a few of the outstanding discoveries which have rendered Baldwin Spencer's work epoch-making in the history of science, because they reveal the mental condition and social activities of man at a lower stage of evolution than any other in which his life has been described for us by competent observers. It is very improbable that any similar revelation of primitive humanity awaits us

in the future ; for the circle of living savagery—
that preserve of ancient man—is rapidly shrinking
through the perpetual encroachments of civilization,
which threatens before long to swallow it up altogether.   Hence the record of Central Australian
savagery, which we owe primarily to the genius of
Baldwin Spencer, is likely to remain for all time
the standard by reference to which, more than to
any other documents, future inquirers will attempt
to estimate the comparative antiquity of forms of
society and to trace them to their origin in times
which lie far beyond the reach of history.   Thus
the work of Spencer promises to provide a firm and
solid basis for all future researches into the early
phases of the mental and social evolution of our
species.

If we ask what were the qualities which enabled
Spencer to accomplish his great work, the answer
would seem to be that they were a lively curiosity
and insatiable thirst for knowledge, first-rate powers
of observation, inexhaustible patience, and an entire
freedom from the bias of preconceived ideas, all
combined with and reposing on an iron will, great
capacity of physical endurance, and a genial and
cheerful disposition, which won him the confidence
and esteem of the shy savages, who treated him as
one of themselves, recognized him as a full member
of the tribe, and revealed to him secrets which they
would probably have concealed from a less sympathetic inquirer.   Hence in all his wanderings,
though they brought him into contact with natives
of whom some had never seen a European before,
while others had been engaged in bloody affrays

with white men, his relations with the aborigines were invariably peaceful and friendly ; he never had to resort to his weapons in self-defence.

The openness of a mind unwarped by preconceived notions and foregone conclusions, which is one of Spencer's foremost characteristics, is conspicuous in all his writings and contributes largely to their scientific value. For the most part he was content to record in clear and simple language the facts which he had personally observed or ascertained directly from his native informants ; he did not attempt to theorize upon them or to institute comparisons between them and those of other peoples in other parts of the world. All such theories and comparisons he regularly and rightly left to the comparative ethnologist, whose function is at once different from and complementary to that of the descriptive ethnologist.

Perhaps the only subject on which Spencer, departing for once from his habitual reserve, indulged in speculation on origins, was that of the Classificatory System of Relationship. This curious system, which may perhaps be described as the hall-mark of savagery, since it appears to be universally prevalent among savage tribes and universally absent among civilized peoples, arranges all the members of a community in classes or groups on the basis of their social rather than consanguineous relations to each other. Spencer found it in full vogue among the Arunta and the other Australian tribes with which he came into contact, and after describing it in *The Native Tribes of Central Australia* (published jointly with F. J. Gillen) he adduced some reasons for thinking that this system of group relationship was derived from a system of group marriage, of which he believed traces to survive in certain existing customs regulating the relations of the sexes among the Australian aborigines. But when he treated of the same subject in his later work, *The Arunta*, which is in substance a revised and enlarged edition of the account which he had given of that tribe in *The Native Tribes of Central Australia*, he entirely omitted this suggestion as to the origin of the Classificatory System of Relationship, and confined himself to describing the facts of the system in a fuller form, leaving his readers to draw their own inferences. Apparently he had come to the conclusion that the discussion of origins should form no part of the description of a particular tribe. But I have no reason to think that he ever abandoned the theory, for he vigorously maintained it in a personal discussion with Professor Edward Westermarck which took place at my rooms in the Temple long after the publication of *The Native Tribes of Central Australia*, but before the publication of *The Arunta*. Elsewhere in his writings, so far as I remember, he has uniformly abstained from the discussion of origins, and in so doing he has given proof of his scientific caution. The whole bent of his mind was indeed to observation rather than to speculation ; he collected an immense mass of new and important facts, but in general he left the interpretation of them to others. He laid the foundations of the science of man in a series of exact observations ; it will be for future inquirers to complete the structure by rearing on his foundations a solid edifice compacted of sound inductions. That may prove a task which will demand the labours of generations yet to come.

Among the high qualities which Spencer brought to the execution of his life work we ought not to overlook his artistic temperament and skill. He derived the keenest enjoyment from the contemplation of beautiful pictures, and would spend whole days in the great European galleries feasting his eyes on their masterpieces. Indeed, these galleries were among the magnets which drew him most strongly from Australia to Europe. During the Great War he even risked his life by crossing the submarine-infested seas to visit London for the purpose of procuring pictures for the Art Gallery at Melbourne, in which he took a deep interest. He was himself no mean draughtsman, and used to illustrate his journals and family letters profusely with sketches which testify alike to the keenness of his observation and to the deftness of his hand. Many of these sketches are reproduced in the last work which he published, *Wanderings in Wild Australia*, and they help the reader greatly to picture to his mind's eye the scenes described by the explorer.

But still more graphic than his sketches are the verbal descriptions which Spencer gives of the varied and often wonderful regions which he traversed in his immense journeys ; for he wielded the pen no less adroitly than the pencil, and the landscapes which he depicts for us, while they never seek literary effect by elaborate word-painting, always bear the impress of perfect fidelity to nature. A conspicuous instance of his descriptive power is his account of the marvellous change which comes over the Australian desert when a drought of many months is broken by heavy rain, and what had seemed a region of absolute sterility and death is suddenly transformed, as if by magic, into a vast garden gay with a profusion of flowering plants and teeming with an endless variety of animal life. The same power of bringing a landscape vividly before the reader's mind comes out in his incidental descriptions alike of the dreary stony plains, desolate mountains, and rocky gorges of the far interior, and of the lily pools and tangled thickets of the northerly regions, where a more abundant supply of moisture and the neighbourhood of the sea lend to the country a softer and more luxuriant aspect, which contrasts sharply with the stern and forbidding character of the central desert. And everywhere, with an artist's eye, he notes the colours of flowers and trees, of birds and beasts, of sky and cloud, which relieve and brighten what is too often the dull and featureless monotony of the bleak Australian scenery.

It is true that the author's powers of landscape painting find little scope in his purely anthropological works, where his attention is concentrated on the natives themselves rather than on their natural surroundings, but they impart vividness to the narrative of his travels in his latest book, *Wanderings in Wild Australia*. In the directness and simplicity of its style, in the impression which it leaves of truth to nature, in the fascination of its descriptions of strange folk and ever shifting scenery, *Wanderings in Wild Australia* may be compared to the *Odyssey*. If the writer did not tread enchanted ground, at least he moved among people who firmly believed in the power of enchantment and constantly resorted to it for the satisfaction of their wants and the confusion of their foes ; if he did not encounter monsters like the Cyclopes or Scylla and Charybdis, at least he beheld with his own eyes the rocky pool in which the dreadful dragon, the Wollunqua, was believed to lurk, ready to dart out and devour its human victims. All this serves to invest the story of Spencer's wanderings in Australia with an atmosphere of romance, and to lend it the character of an anthropological epic.

The same restless and untiring pursuit of knowledge which led this knight-errant of science to undertake these wanderings led him at the end of his life to extend his researches to another continent and another people, the aborigines of Tierra del Fuego. It was a gallant attempt, but the weaker body refused to bear the last burden laid on it by the indomitable spirit. His wanderings are now over, and he rests from his labours, far from his native England and his friends, in a lonely grave under the southern stars. But his writings will long survive him for the enlightenment of a distant posterity and for a monument, more lasting than any of bronze or marble, to his fame.

CANON JOHN ROSCOE

(From *Nature*, 17th December 1932, pp. 917-919)

V

CANON JOHN ROSCOE

WHEN in the nineties of last century I had the great good fortune to make the acquaintance of my valued friend, the late Canon John Roscoe, he was settled as a missionary of the Church Missionary Society among the Baganda, the great tribe or nation which has given its name to Uganda, in Central Africa. But he had previously resided in the same capacity for some years in that part of East Africa now called Tanganyika, which was afterwards taken over by Germany and known as German East Africa. Of his life in that country and his observations of the native tribes he has given a brief account in a volume published long afterwards, *Twenty-five Years in East Africa*. The account includes the notice of a curious form of human sacrifice practised by the natives which he succeeded in suppressing. He left the country at the time when the Germans took possession of it, and falling into the hands of the Arabs, who opposed the German invasion, he and his wife narrowly escaped being put to death by their captors, the messenger who brought their ransom only arriving about an hour before the time fixed for their execution.

It was not until he settled among the Baganda, however, that Roscoe began systematically to in-

vestigate and record the customs and beliefs of the
natives among whom he lived. The results of his
observations were first published in a series of valuable articles in the *Journal of the Anthropological
Institute*, which are perhaps not wholly superseded
by his systematic work on the subject, *The Baganda*,
which appeared some years later, in 1911. In his
researches among the Baganda, he received important aid from his friend, the native prime
minister of Uganda, who was not only himself
versed in the lore of his people but also brought
as informants from all parts of the country old
men acquainted from their youth with the ancient
traditions and customs which even then, at the
beginning of the twentieth century, had passed or
were passing out of use and even out of memory.
Thus by his timely intervention, and the efficient
help of his native informants, Roscoe was able to
put on record a large body of information on the old
life of the Baganda which otherwise would inevitably
have been lost to science. His writings on the
Baganda must therefore remain for all time the
standard authority on that important tribe, one of
the most powerful and most politically developed of
all the Bantu peoples.

While his researches were in the main concentrated on the Baganda, Roscoe's anthropological
enthusiasm, which never flagged, led him to extend
his investigations to many other peoples of the
Uganda Protectorate. He availed himself of his
holidays to visit and examine some of them, particularly the Banyoro (or Bakitara), the Banyankole, and the Basoga, all of whose territories border

on that of the Baganda, as well as other and more
distant tribes, including the savage and cannibal
Bagesu, on the slopes of the lofty Mount Elgon.
The scientific results of these excursions he published in *The Northern Bantu*, a volume replete
with interesting information concerning these tribes,
about which comparatively little had been previously
known.

Even after Roscoe had returned to England in
1909 and was living in his quiet rural rectory at
Ovington, near Thetford, in Norfolk, to which, in
recognition of his eminent services to science, he
had been presented by the University of Cambridge
in 1912, his interest in these tribes of Central Africa
remained unabated, and he longed to revisit them
and push his investigations farther among them and
among fresh tribes as yet untouched by European
influence. Representations made on his behalf to
the Government to enable him to undertake an
expedition for this purpose were sympathetically
received by Mr. Harcourt, then at the head of the
Colonial Office, but they finally came to nothing.
At last, after the War, his opportunity came, when
the enlightened munificence of the late Sir Peter
Mackie furnished him with the means of carrying
out the wish of his heart. The funds provided by
the generous donor were administered by a committee of the Royal Society, under the auspices of
which Roscoe set out in 1919, and after spending
about a year in the field returned in 1920. He hus-
banded his resources and secured complete freedom
of movement by travelling alone except for the
necessary bearers. It had been his wish and in-

tention to examine the almost unknown tribes in
the north-east, between Lake Rudolf and the southern border of Abyssinia, but unfortunately political
complications in that region compelled him to
abandon this important part of his programme, and
that part of the ethnographical survey still remains
undone, though I understand that there is some
prospect of the blank being supplied before long
by a younger investigator.

Thus restricted in the scope of his inquiries,
Roscoe was obliged to retrace his steps over what
to him was, in some measure, beaten ground.   Still
he made, in his year of absence, a wide circuit of
the Protectorate, revisited his old friends the Banyankole, the Banyoro, the Bagesu, and the Basoga,
and collected much additional information about
them, besides breaking fresh ground among new
and almost unknown tribes on the wilds of the lofty
Mount Ruwenzori and elsewhere.   The scientific
results of his expedition were published by the
Cambridge University Press in three volumes, *The
Bakitara or Banyoro*, *The Banyankole*, and *The
Bagesu*.   He also published a more popular account
of the expedition under the title of *The Soul of
Central Africa*, in which descriptions of the native
tribes are agreeably varied by graphic descriptions
of scenery and incidents of travel—personal details
which he always rigidly and rightly excluded from
his strictly scientific writings.

On this expedition Roscoe devoted most time to
the Banyoro or Bakitara as the most important and
formerly most powerful tribe of the Protectorate
after the Baganda.   In his inquiries among them

he received much help from the native king, who
took great interest in the work and was at pains
to supply Roscoe with the fullest and most authentic
information. Thus my friend was enabled to do
for the Banyoro what he had already done for the
Baganda, to supply a great African tribe with an
accurate account of its present state and past history, so far as these could be ascertained by personal observation and the most trustworthy native
tradition.

As a field anthropologist, Roscoe had in his day
few equals and probably no superior. He was a
first-rate observer, with a keen sense of what is
important and deserving of record ; entirely free
from theoretical bias, he always contented himself
with stating in clear and simple language the results
of his observations and inquiries ; for him it was
enough to record the facts ; he did not attempt to
explain them by his own or other people's theories.
Still less did he fall into the trap, into which too
many field anthropologists have tumbled, by com-
paring his African facts with facts raked together
from all the ends of the earth : all such explanations
and comparisons he rightly left to be elaborated by
comparative anthropologists at home working in
libraries on the reports of field ethnologists like himself. As one of these workers at home who have
profited immensely by his researches in the field,
the results of which he freely and generously com-
municated to me by letter and word of mouth as
well as in his published writings, I desire to place on
record my sense of the deep debt of gratitude under
which he has laid all students of ethnology by his

long and devoted labours in Central Africa. As documents of first-rate authority on the tribes of the Uganda Protectorate, his writings can never be superseded ; they will remain imperishable monuments of the people and of the man.

But while his writings attest to the world the tenacity of purpose and the strength and keenness of the intellectual powers which enabled Roscoe to accomplish his great work under all the distractions of a laborious profession, and all the difficulties and hardships of long journeys performed in a tropical climate, for the most part in days when modern facilities of travel were still unknown, only his intimates knew the kindly sympathetic nature which endeared him to his friends and won the hearts of his dusky flock in Africa, as afterwards of his parishioners at home in England.

Of that, however, it is for others to speak. But it would be wrong to conclude this brief and imperfect notice of Canon Roscoe's anthropological work without directing attention to one feature of it which added greatly to its value. All his information, I believe, was obtained directly from natives in their own language without the aid of interpreters, his own long and intimate familiarity with Bantu speech enabling him to dispense with those dangerous intermediaries in all his intercourse with the Bantu tribes who form the great bulk of the inhabitants of the Uganda Protectorate. Thus his reports of native customs and beliefs are entirely exempt from one most fruitful source of doubt, ambiguity, and error which infests and tends to corrupt and falsify all testimony in passing through the medium of an interpreter, who, even if he be honest, may unconsciously pervert the purport of the communication he is charged to make through his imperfect acquaintance with one or both of the languages of which, as a go-between, he is obliged to make use. Readers of Canon Roscoe's works have, therefore, the satisfaction of knowing that the stream of his discourse flows pure and clear from native sources, unsullied by passing through the too often turbid and weedy channel of an intermediary.

CONDORCET ON THE PROGRESS OF THE HUMAN MIND

(The Zaharoff Lecture at Oxford for 1933)

VI

CONDORCET ON THE PROGRESS OF
THE HUMAN MIND

OF all the philosophers and economists of the eighteenth century who by their writings and personal
influence prepared the minds of men for the French
Revolution and cast the mould into which the
burning lava of that tremendous eruption finally
ran and solidified, Condorcet alone survived to reap
in death the fruit—the bitter fruit—of which he had
sowed the seeds by his life. He lived to witness the
whole of the great drama from its overture in the
assembling of the States-General and the fall of
the Bastille in 1789 to its culmination in the Reign
of Terror in 1794. He was not a mere spectator
of it; as a member at first of the municipality of
Paris and afterwards of the Legislative Assembly
and the Convention, he played a prominent and
important part on the political stage ; and under
the shadow of the guillotine, of which he escaped—
and barely escaped—the falling axe, he wrote during
the last months of his life what we may call his
political testament or apology, in which with un-
shaken confidence and imperturbable serenity he
not only defended the principles of the Revolution
but proclaimed by anticipation their extension to

the rest of Europe and ultimately to the whole
civilized world, ushering in, as with a blast of angel
trumpets, the dawn of a new era of enlightenment, of
justice, and of peace and goodwill upon earth.   The
testimony of such a man to the Revolution is in
the highest degree interesting and instructive.   For
he was no vulgar demagogue, no ignorant upstart,
inflamed with hatred of his social superiors and
burning to drag them down to his own low level ; an
aristocrat by birth and, we may add, by temper and
feeling, a man of science by deliberate choice and
long devotion to abstract studies, the Marquis of
Condorcet (for a Marquis he was) may be reckoned,
like the Gracchi at Rome, among the finest examples of men of noble birth who, with a fervour
and a passion still nobler than their birth, have
consecrated all their powers to succouring the weak,
relieving the oppressed, and spreading the light of
knowledge over the world for the improvement and
enrichment of humanity.   For of Condorcet it has
been well said that, if he was by predilection a
mathematician, a philosopher, and an economist,
he was first and foremost by nature a philanthropist,
a friend of mankind.

The document in which Condorcet recorded his
views of the French Revolution and essayed to
trace in broad outline the progress of humanity in
the past and to forecast its course in the future has
now, after the lapse of nearly a century and a half,
a twofold interest for us, since it sheds a light, a
lurid light, not only on the epoch of the Revolution
but on the times in which we live.   For we of this
generation and of the generation which is passing

away have witnessed, and indeed are still witnessing, though happily at a safe distance, a revolution in Russia which presents many points of similarity to the first great Revolution in France. The words of fiery eloquence in which Edmund Burke, the wisest of political thinkers, branded the Jacobins of his day are applicable, with hardly a change but that of names, to the Bolsheviks of our day. In Russia of to-day, as in France of the day before yesterday, we see the same systematic and determined attacks on those institutions which hitherto had been regarded as the very pillars of civilized society ; I mean the institutions of private property, the family, and religion ; we see the destruction of these institutions proclaimed as a new gospel to be preached to all nations, established at home by wholesale confiscations, robberies, murders, and massacres, and propagated abroad to the ends of the earth by the apostles and emissaries of disorder, sedition, and civil war. And like the Revolution in France this monstrous brood of political locusts has been hatched in the brains of a few purely speculative thinkers or dreamers, whose glaring fallacies, though they have often been exposed and refuted,[1] still furnish plausible demagogues and glib mountebanks with levers whereby to turn the world upside down. For unhappily in the scales of human judgement the clear dictates of reason are too often outweighed by the blind impulse of the passions.

But from the gloomy spectacle of the thunder-

[1] Notably by the late Professor R. Flint (*Socialism*, London, 1895) and Professor F. J. C. Hearnshaw (*A Survey of Socialism*, London, 1928).

cloud, pregnant with infernal fire, which now in Europe darkens the eastern horizon and threatens to engulf the whole heavens, it is a relief to turn for a little to the bright, if visionary, picture of the future of humanity which Condorcet painted, like a great fresco on a prison wall, in his *Sketch of an Historical Picture of the Progress of the Human Mind*, the work which he bequeathed, almost with his last breath, to posterity for their guidance and encouragement even in the darkest hours that can overtake a nation or an individual.

But before we pass to a consideration of that remarkable work it may be well to look a little closer at the life and character of the writer, since these are always the determining factors in the composition of a book.

Jean Antoine Nicolas Caritat, Marquis of Condorcet, was born at the little town of Ribemont on the 17th of September 1743.[1] The Caritats were an ancient and noble family in the south of France. Originally they belonged to the principality of Orange, but towards the middle of the sixteenth century they migrated to the south of Dauphiné. Their castle, near Nyons, passed into the possession of Henri de Caritat by his marriage with Sebastienne de Poitiers. An ardent and passionate race, the Caritats embraced the Reformed Faith and defended

[1] For the life of Condorcet I have relied chiefly on the general biography by Arago prefixed to his edition of Condorcet's works (vol. i., Paris, 1847-1848, pp. iii-clxxi) and the elaborate political biography by Léon Cahen (*Condorcet et la Révolution française*, Paris, 1904), who made researches among the unpublished papers of Condorcet in the library of the Institut at Paris, the National Archives, and elsewhere.

it obstinately for forty years, after which, in the
seventeenth century, they abandoned it and reverted
to Catholicism, but by their successive changes of
religious profession they gained nothing in the way
of honours and fortune.   In the eighteenth century,
under changed conditions, they retained their ancient
characteristics of pride and independence.   Neither
riches nor progress appear to have had any attrac-
tions for them.   They were nobles and kept the
prejudices of their order.   Their favourite profession was that of arms.[1]   Condorcet's father was a
captain of cavalry, and when in his youth Condorcet decided to devote himself to mathematics
there was only one of his family who forgave him
for not choosing to be a cavalry officer like his
father before him.[2]   But some of Condorcet's
family entered the Church, and rose to high office
in it.   His father's elder brother was successively
bishop of Gap, of Auxerre, and of Lisieux, and
exerted himself to re-establish order in his diocese
with an energy and even brutality which procured
for him many bitter enemies in his lifetime.[3]   His
father dying when Condorcet was barely four years
old, the care of the child devolved on his mother,
a devout and superstitious lady, who, to guard her
young son from the perils of infancy, dedicated him
to the Virgin and dressed him as a girl.   For eight
years the boy wore the costume of a girl, and in the
opinion of the biographers the dress, by preventing
him from taking active bodily exercise, impeded

[1] L. Cahen, *Condorcet et la
Révolution française*, pp. 3 *sq.*
[2] Arago, *Biographie*, pp. vi,
xxxi.
[3] L. Cahen, *op. cit.* p. 4;
Arago, *Biographie*, pp. vi-vii.

his growth and impaired his health for the rest of his life.[1]   But we may doubt whether the supposed cause could have produced such an effect. More legitimate, perhaps, is the conjecture that the girlish dress was intended by the mother to guard her little son against the Evil Eye; for in India to this day it is said to be a common custom to dress boys as girls for that purpose, the notion apparently being that the disguise deceives and foils the powers of evil.[2]

From the tutelage of his tender but too anxious mother Condorcet passed into the charge of his uncle, the bishop of Lisieux, who provided him with a Jesuit tutor and afterwards sent him to a Jesuit College at Rheims, from which in 1758 he passed to another Jesuit institution, the College of Navarre at Paris. The education which he received from the Jesuit Fathers seems to have exercised little influence on Condorcet except in the way of strong revulsion; in later life he severely criticized their system of instruction.[3]   After leaving the College of Navarre, Condorcet resolved to devote himself to geometry. The resolution was strenuously opposed by his family, but he was firm, and after a long struggle they gave way. Thus left free to follow his bent, the young man settled down to a quiet studious life in the Rue Jacob at Paris, going little into society and working at mathematics, it is said, for ten hours a day.[4]   At this period of his life

---

[1] Arago, *Biographie*, p. vii; L Cahen, *op. cit.* p. 5.

[2] J. G. Frazer, *Garnered Sheaves* (London, 1931), pp. 165 *sq.*

[3] Arago, *Biographie*, pp. vii-ix ; L. Cahen, *op. cit.* pp. 5 *sq.*

[4] I.. Cahen, *op. cit.* p. 7.

he is described by Madame de l'Espinasse as a great hulking gawky youth, shy and embarrassed in manner, who walked stooping, bit his nails, blushed when spoken to, and either said nothing in reply or spoke low and fast.[1] This shyness and awkwardness in society the philosopher seems to have retained to the end of his life. But under a somewhat cold and reserved exterior there beat a warm heart. His friend d'Alembert described him as a volcano covered with snow.[2] In his youth he gave proof of the tenderness of his heart by renouncing the pastime of hunting, to which he was passionately attached, because he would not wantonly inflict pain on animals ; he even refrained from killing insects, unless they hurt him very much.[3] It seems a strange contradiction in human nature that the same man who exhibited an almost Buddhistic tenderness for animal life should afterwards have sat as a judge at the Bloody Assize of the Convention, which sent so many hundreds of innocent human victims to the scaffold.

Condorcet's mathematical studies early attracted the attention and received the compliments of d'Alembert, Clairaut, and Fontaine, who saluted him as their future colleague in the Academy of Science.[4] Soon afterwards, at the age of barely twenty-two, he composed an *Essay on the Integral Calculus*, which he presented to the Academy.[5] With the numerous other mathematical memoirs which he produced, it was highly appreciated by

[1] L. Cahen, *ibid.*
[2] Arago, *Biographie*, pp. clxi
sq.
[3] *Ibid.* p. xi.
[4] *Ibid.* p. ix.
[5] *Ibid.* p. xiii.

the great mathematicians, Lagrange and d'Alembert.[1] In 1778 Condorcet divided with Tempelhoff a prize offered by the Berlin Academy for determining the orbits of comets.[2] He had already been elected a member of the Academy of Science in 1769,[3] and later he succeeded Fouchy as Secretary of the Academy, an office which he held till his death. In it, as an official duty, he composed many obituary notices of deceased members of the Academy.[4] To the composition of these eulogistic notices (*éloges*) Condorcet may have in part owed his election to the French Academy in 1782, when, after a sharp contest, he beat his rival candidate, the unfortunate astronomer Bailly, by a single vote. Little could the rivals in this honourable competition foresee that, before many years had passed, one of them was to perish in a prison and the other on the scaffold. D'Alembert rejoiced at Condorcet's election. The aged Voltaire had long desired it, and had even humorously threatened that, if his wish were not gratified, he would go and pass the rest of his youth at the Academy of Berlin or the Academy of St. Petersburg.[5]

But long before the date of his election to the French Academy Condorcet had turned his attention seriously to social, ethical, and economic questions. In a letter to Turgot of 1775 he wrote that at the age of seventeen he had meditated on the ideas of justice and virtue and on the problem of how our own personal interest enjoins us to be just and

[1] Arago, *Biographie*, p. xv.
[2] *Ibid.* pp. xix *sq.*
[3] *Ibid.* p. xxxi.
[4] *Ibid.* pp. xlii *sq.*
[5] *Ibid.* pp. lxxxviii-xc.

virtuous.[1] Early convinced of the indefinite perfectibility of humanity, he conceived the promotion
of human progress to be one of the sweetest occupa-
tions and one of the first duties of every man who
has fortified his reason by study and meditation.[2]
In thus directing his mind to the practical amelioration of human life Condorcet was doubtless influenced in large measure by his friendship with the
great economist and wise statesman, Turgot, with
whose views on political economy, and especially
on the benefits of free trade, he was in entire sympathy and agreement.[3] Both men, too, were at one
on the question of the natural rights of man and
the freedom of the individual ; both were declared
enemies of slavery.[4] Hence when in 1774 Turgot
was created Minister of Finance he appointed
Condorcet to the office of Inspector of Moneys or,
as we should say, Master of the Mint,[5] and he also
named him to be one of a Commission of Three
(d'Alembert and Bossut being the other two members) charged with the duty of reporting on a vast
scheme for improving the inland navigation of
France by the construction of canals to link up the
principal rivers ; it may be added that, to their
honour, all three members of the Commission refused
to accept the salaries offered them by the minister.[6]
But these and all the other fine schemes which the
fertile brain of the wise minister had struck out for
the salvation of France were shattered by the speedy
dismissal of Turgot from office and his replacement

[1] *Ibid.* p. x.
[2] *Ibid.* p. xxvii.
[3] *Ibid.* pp. lxviii-lxix.
[4] *Ibid.* pp. lxix-lxxi.
[5] *Ibid.* p. lxxi.
[6] *Ibid.* pp. lxxii-lxxiv.

by Necker, under whose misguided policy the drift towards the precipice of Revolution became every day more rapid. When Necker published a pamphlet opposing the free circulation of corn in France, Condorcet replied to it in an anonymous *Letter of a Labourer in Picardy* which received the warm approval of Voltaire. Afterwards in a memoir entitled *Reflections on the Corn-trade* he discussed the whole question more at large, upholding the advantages of free trade in corn in opposition to Necker's policy of maintaining the old restrictions. The memoir excited the bitter resentment of Necker and his partisans; and in these circumstances Condorcet, feeling it impossible to retain office under the offended minister, resigned his post of Inspector of Moneys.[1] Looking back on the too short period of hope during which Turgot had been at the helm of government in France, Condorcet wrote to Voltaire: "We have had a beautiful dream, but it was too brief. I am about to return to geometry. It is cold comfort to labour for paltry glory after flattering oneself for a time that one was working for the public good."[2]

But when in 1789 the Revolution at last broke out, Condorcet eagerly grasped what he believed to be the supreme opportunity of working for the public good, and plunged headlong into the revolutionary whirlpool. He was elected a member of the municipality of Paris, and afterwards in 1791 became one of six commissioners of the National Treasury.[3] A little later he was chosen member of the Legis-

---

[1] Arago, *Biographie*, pp. lxxiv-lxxix.   [2] *Ibid*. pp. xxvii-xxviii.
[3] *Ibid*. pp. civ, cvii.

lative Assembly, of which he was at first one of
the secretaries and afterwards the President.[1] In the
Legislative Assembly Condorcet moved that all
patents of nobility throughout France should be
burned.   The motion was carried unanimously, and
accordingly, on the 19th of June 1792, a great pile
of these documents was burnt at the foot of the
statue of Louis XIV.; among them no doubt Condorcet's own patent of marquisate helped to feed the
flames.[2] Though he took no part in the personal
quarrels which raged in the Legislative Assembly,
Condorcet was elected member of the Convention
by five different constituencies.[3] At the trial of
Louis XVI. in the Convention, Condorcet maintained that the Assembly had no legal right to try
the king, and that in virtue of the Constitution the
monarch was inviolable.   Nevertheless, he voted
at the trial, but not for the sentence of death; he
declared in favour of an appeal to the people.[4]

On the 11th of October 1792 the Convention
appointed a Committee of Nine to draw up a project
of a new Constitution for France.   Condorcet was
one of the members chosen to serve on it, and
among the other members were Danton, Siéyès,
and the Englishman, Tom Paine.   Robespierre had
hoped to be one of the members, and is said to have
bitterly resented his exclusion.[5]   After four months
of labour the Committee presented its scheme of a
new Constitution to the Convention on the 15th of

---

[1] *Ibid.* p. cix.
[2] *Ibid.* p. cxiii.
[3] *Ibid.* pp. cxv-cxvii.
[4] *Ibid.* pp. cxvii-cxxiii.

[5] *Ibid.* pp. cxxiii *sqq.*; L.
Cahen, *Condorcet et la Révolution française*, p. 467.

February 1793 ; the chief authors of the scheme are said to have been Condorcet and Tom Paine. Their report was coldly received by the Assembly, and after long and stormy debates the scheme was finally shelved without being put to the vote. Later on the Convention charged the Committee of Public Safety, reinforced by five members, to draw up another plan of Constitution. On the 10th of June 1793 this new plan was submitted to the Convention, and on the 24th of June it was accepted almost without discussion.[1] Indignant at this decision of the Convention, which had accepted a hasty project almost without examination, Condorcet resolved to protest publicly against it. With this view he wrote anonymously a letter of *Advice to the French on the New Constitution*, which he caused to be secretly printed and circulated to the departments. In this letter he exposed the defects of the proposed new Constitution unsparingly, and exhorted all good citizens to reject it.[2]

The secret of the authorship of the letter leaked out, and the Convention treated it as an act of high treason. Accordingly, on the 8th of July 1793, Chabot, a bitter enemy of Condorcet, denounced him to the Convention, which decreed his accusation and ordered his arrest. The officers at once attempted to execute the order, first at Condorcet's town house in the Rue de Lille, at the corner of the Rue Belle Chasse, and afterwards at his country house in Auteuil, but at both houses he was absent. For he had received a timely warning from his

---

[1] Arago, *op. cit.* pp. cxxiii *sqq.*;   [2] Arago, *op. cit.* pp. cxxvi *sq.* ;
L. Cahen, *op. cit.* pp. 467-521.   L. Cahen, *op. cit.* pp. 522 *sq.*

friend, the doctor Cabanis, and acting on it had
taken refuge in the house of Madame Vernet, No.
21 (now 15) Rue Servandoni, a quiet street leading
down from the gardens of the Luxembourg to the
stately church of St. Sulpice.[1] Madame Vernet,
the widow of a sculptor, kept lodgings for students
and had been prepared by friends of Condorcet to
receive him. Without naming him they had asked
her whether she would shelter a proscribed man.
Her reply was, " Is he a good man ? " and when
they said, " Yes ", " Let him come at once ", she
answered, " you will tell me his name afterwards.
Lose not a minute. Even while we speak your
friend may be arrested." So he came late in the
evening of that July day, and for nine months this
noble-minded woman sheltered him in her house at
the peril of her life.[2] She well knew the risks she
ran ; for in the streets at her door bills posted on the
walls denounced in large letters the penalty of death
on all who harboured the proscribed.[3] It is true
that at the time when Condorcet took refuge with
her he was as yet only accused, not condemned, but
the condemnation followed a few months later, when
on the 3rd of October 1793 he was tried by the
revolutionary tribunal on a charge of conspiring
against the unity of the Republic, and in his absence
was condemned to death and his property confiscated.[4]

So long as he stayed in the house of Madame
Vernet the philosopher was safe, but uneasy at the

---

[1] Arago, *op. cit.* pp. cxxvii
sq., cxxxiii *sq.* ; L. Cahen, *op.
cit.* pp. 523-525.

[2] Arago, *op. cit.* pp. cxxxiii

sq. ; L. Cahen, *op. cit.* pp. 525-
527.

[3] Arago, *Biographie*, p. cliii.

[4] *Ibid.* pp. cxxviii *sq.*

danger in which he involved his generous hostess
he meditated flight, though she and even the portress,
who was in the secret, kept a strict watch on him
to prevent his departure.   At last, alarmed by a
mysterious warning which he had received of a
threatened domiciliary visit, he contrived to evade
their vigilance, and on the morning of the 5th of
April 1794, imperfectly disguised, he brushed past
the portress and issued on the street.   He had only
taken a few steps when at the corner of the neighbouring Rue Vaugirard he was met and recognized
by a cousin of Madame Vernet, who, bravely in-
different to his own danger, guided him past the
sentinels at the gates into the open country.   There
the forlorn philosopher wandered for two days without food or shelter, till, late in the afternoon of the
third day, driven by the pangs of hunger, he entered
a humble tavern at Clamart and called for an
omelette.   Asked how many eggs he would have
in it, he answered at random, " Twelve ".   The
reply excited suspicion and he was asked for his
papers, but he had none, only a copy of the *Epistles*
of Horace.   So the police were sent for; he was
arrested and marched off to Bourg-la-Reine, where
he was put in prison.   Next morning when the
gaoler entered his cell to send him under guard to
Paris, they found him lying dead on the floor.   The
cause of his death is uncertain.   The common tradition, accepted by his biographer Arago, is that
he died of a strong dose of poison which for some
time he had carried about with him in a ring.[1]   But

---

[1] Arago, *Biographie*, pp. cli-
clvii.   The story of his last days
is told with some variations of
detail by Condorcet's other bio-

against this view it has been urged, with much force, that the medical officer, who examined his body, certified that he died of a congestion of the blood (*congestion sanguine*), without any mention of poison, and that at Clamart the prisoner had been carefully searched and stripped of all his possessions, including his watch, pocket-book, pocket-knife, razor, and the volume of Horace ; it is unlikely, therefore, that the ring should have eluded the search. Condorcet was of a delicate constitution, and bodily fatigue, combined with hunger, cold, and exposure, during his two days of homeless wandering, to say nothing of his mental anguish, seem sufficient to account for his tragic death, without resorting to the hypothesis of poison. So weak, indeed, was he at the moment of his arrest that a cart had to be fetched to transport him to prison at Bourg-la-Reine, or Bourg-Egalité as the place was called in the Jacobin jargon.[1] It is no matter of wonder if, under such a load of suffering, exhausted nature should have finally broken down that same night.

To beguile the tedious hours and to dispel the heavy thoughts which might well have oppressed a mind less erect and noble than his own during his long seclusion in the Rue Servandoni, Condorcet set himself to compose his *Sketch of an Historical Picture of the Progress of the Human Mind*,[2] the

grapher, L. Cahen, *op. cit.* pp. 537-541. According to him, the date when Condorcet quitted his refuge in the Rue Servandoni was the fifth day of Germinal in the year II of the Republic, that is, 25th March 1794. I follow Arago without presuming to settle minor differences between the biographers.

[1] L. Cahen, *op. cit.* pp. 540-541.

[2] Printed in Condorcet, *Œuvres*, publiées par A. Condorcet O'Connor et M. F. Arago, vol. vi. (Paris, 1847). On this treatise I

work by which he is now chiefly remembered.   To
it we must now turn our attention.

The work is much more than a revolutionary
manifesto—the profession of faith of a republican
who beheld with joy the sweeping away of the
hereditary monarchy which towards the end of
his life he had come to regard as a fatal clog on
progress.   It is a philosophical, if not wholly dis-
passionate, disquisition on the nature of man, a bold
attempt to sketch the whole of his history from
his humble origin in the past and to forecast his
glorious destiny in the future.   It abounds in deep
thoughts and fruitful suggestions : it raises questions
which still agitate the minds of men and may long
continue to perplex them : it anticipates several
conclusions which modern science has either proved
or rendered highly probable ; and while it points
to certain existing or threatened evils of far-reaching
significance, it suggests some remedies or palliatives
which civilized societies have since adopted or may
be driven to adopt hereafter.   It may interest my
hearers to have a few of these pregnant thoughts
succinctly laid before them.   To weigh them in the
critical balance would exceed both the time at my
disposal and the range of my knowledge.

In the first place, then, Condorcet accepted with
enthusiasm and conviction the doctrine of the in-
finite perfectibility of human nature which was
current among the French philosophers of the

may refer to my article " Condorcet on Human Progress ",
*The Gorgon's Head and other
Literary Pieces* (London, 1927),
pp. 369-383, from which I have
here allowed myself to borrow
freely.

eighteenth century.[1]   On this point he insists again
and again.   Thus, at the outset of his treatise he
says that he has undertaken to prove by reasoning
and by the evidence of facts, " that nature has set
no bounds to the improvement of human faculties ;
that the perfectibility of man is really indefinite ;
that its progress is henceforth independent of any
power to arrest it, and has no limit but the dura-
tion of the globe on which nature has cast us".[2]
Again he affirms that " the moral goodness of
man, a necessary result of his organism, is, like
all other faculties, susceptible of indefinite perfec-
tionment ".[3]

As a trained man of science, Condorcet recognized and fully accepted the modern conception
of the universal reign of natural law.   The sole
foundation, he says, for the belief in the natural
sciences is the idea that the universe is regulated
by necessary and constant laws ; why then, he asks,
should this principle be less true of the development
of the intellectual and moral faculties of man than
of the other operations of nature ?[4]   That development, he held, has been slow and gradual, beginning
at a rudimentary stage at which man hardly, if at
all, differed from the rest of the animals, and progressing by a regular gradation to the most advanced
civilization of the present day, which is itself merely
a passing phase destined to be far transcended hereafter.   The fundamental kinship of man with the
lower animals, which the theory of evolution has

[1] J. B. Bury, *The Idea of Progress* (London, 1921), p. 214.
[2] Condorcet, *Œuvres*, vi. p.
13 ; cf. pp. 237 *sq*., 251 *sqq*.
[3] *Ibid*. p. 263.
[4] *Ibid*. p. 236.

since so strongly confirmed, is dwelt upon by Condorcet again and again.[1]   Thus, in order to explain the progress of the human species, he says there is no need to fall back on an essential distinction between man and the brutes, to imagine that he is the fortunate possessor of a soul different from theirs.   Animals reason like men ; like men they form abstract ideas, for without abstract ideas reasoning is impossible ; and like men they have moral sentiments, though of a more rudimentary sort.[2]   Again he says that " in following the march of nature in the development of the beings whom she has endowed with sensibility and thought we always find the same faculties in different degrees, the same processes employed with more or less skill : we pass by insensible gradations from the brute to the savage and from the savage to Euler and Newton ".[3]   In short, as he puts it elsewhere, while man stands at the head of the scale of animate being, he still shares the nature and belongs to the family of the beasts.   But if he thus seems to imply, he nowhere explicitly formulates, the modern theory of the evolution of the human species out of lower forms of animal life.

Like Aristotle in antiquity [4] and Darwin and Westermarck in modern times, Condorcet held that the earliest human society was the family, consisting of parents and children, and that the long infancy of the offspring, necessitating prolonged parental care, was a prime source of the institution of marriage

---

[1] Condorcet, *Œuvres*, vi. pp. 289-295, 305 *sq*., 380.

[2] *Ibid.* pp. 293 *sq*., 380.

[3] *Ibid.* p. 346.

[4] Aristotle, *Politics*, i. 1, 3.

and of the development of morality.¹   Like Adam
Smith, he based the moral sentiments on sympathy,
on an instinctive and organic feeling of uneasiness
at sight of the sufferings of others and a consequent
impulse to relieve them.   Without such sympathy
he thought that the life of the family and of society
was impossible.²   He believed that the progress of
civilization, as manifested in the larger social groups,
the invention of the arts, and the growth of morality,
resulted from the natural development of human
faculties and not from a primitive revelation com-
municated by a deity to the ancestors of the race and
handed down by tradition to their descendants.³
In contrast to the opinion of Rousseau, who held,
or professed to hold, that the change from savagery
to civilization was a process of degeneration and
corruption, Condorcet maintained that it involved
an intellectual and moral amelioration of mankind :
he denied that the advance of knowledge is answer-
able for the vices of civilized nations : on the contrary, he argued that it directly contributes to the
progress of morality by enlightening men as to
their true interests, since immoral actions are often
simply the fruit of ignorance, of a failure to understand that the interests of the individual are identical
with the interests of the community.⁴   He promises
that in the course of his survey of human progress
his readers will perceive " that the stormy and painful passage of a rude society to a state of civilization
like that of enlightened and free peoples is by no

¹ Condorcet, *Œuvres*, vi. pp.   ³ *Ibid.* pp. 380 *sq.*
25 *sq.*, 296 *sq.*
    ² *Ibid.* p. 298.   ⁴ *Ibid.* pp. 37 *sq.*

H

means a degeneration of the human species but a necessary crisis in its gradual march towards a future state of absolute perfection. The reader will see ", he continues, " that it is not the increase but the decadence of knowledge which has produced the vices of polished peoples ; and finally that, far from ever corrupting mankind, knowledge has sweetened their temper even when it could not correct their faults or alter their character ".[1]

Consistently with his view that vice is often the effect of ignorance, Condorcet paid much attention to those errors which, in his opinion, have retarded human progress.[2] Acquiescing with his whole heart in the revolutionary creed of his contemporaries, he accepted the watchwords of liberty and equality as summing up the means whereby mankind can most readily attain to the highest state of happiness and perfection ; and by this standard he judged the errors into which they had fallen in the past. Among these errors, and the practical evils which had flowed from them, he reckoned the hereditary transmission of power and the social inequality of women compared with men. Hereditary power, in his opinion, is the source of the slavery under which almost the whole of mankind has groaned : he looked forward to its universal abolition in the future and to the substitution of republics based on the French model, which already, he thought, commended itself to all the enlightened minds of Europe.[3] With regard to the social subjection of women he held that it rested on no natural basis of

---

[1] Condorcet, *Œuvres*, vi. p. 38.

[2] *Ibid.* pp. 21 *sq.*, 362 *sqq.*

[3] *Ibid.* pp. 364 *sqq.*

a physical, intellectual, or moral difference between the sexes : he declared roundly that it was a sheer abuse of force, which no sophism could justify : he affirmed that in the past it had acted injuriously on the general happiness, including that of the men themselves, and that the equalization of the rights of men and women would be one of the most important and most beneficial features of progress in the future.[1] Subsequent history has gone far to justify his prediction of the legal equalization of the sexes.

Another of the disastrous errors which has retarded the progress of mankind he believed to be religion. On this subject the humane and gentle Condorcet was as fierce and uncompromising an iconoclast as Lucretius himself, as firmly convinced of the countless and unspeakable calamities which faith in the supernatural had inflicted on a suffering humanity.[2] The earliest of all savage superstitions, according to him, was a belief in the survival of the human soul after death,[3] and the second was the belief in gods, whom man created in his own image, for what other model could he have chosen ? [4] While men are naturally disposed by their emotional temperament and analogical reasoning to adopt these two fundamental articles of the religious creed, this natural disposition has been greatly strengthened by the teaching of priests, who, though their leisure enabled them to make some advances in natural science, and particularly in astronomy, purposely

[1] *Ibid.* pp. 263 *sq.*, 303.   [3] *Ibid.* pp. 371 *sq.*
[2] *Ibid.* pp. 29 *sq.*   [4] *Ibid.* pp. 373 *sq.*

refrained from enlightening the ignorant masses by their superior knowledge ; or rather they imparted only so much of it, and in so debased and corrupt a form, to their simple fellows as seemed likely to retain them in a state of servile subjection to their spiritual guides and directors. For the real aims of these priestly sages, according to Condorcet, was not to advance the boundaries of knowledge, but to acquire an absolute control, for their own selfish ends, over the minds of the multitude ; they sought truth only to diffuse error, so we need not wonder that they seldom discovered it. By mixing an element of the supernatural and the miraculous in all their teaching they pandered to the credulity and inflamed the superstitions of the vulgar, that they themselves might be regarded as superior to common humanity, as invested with a sacred char-acter, as the vehicles of a divine revelation dis-closed to themselves and denied to all the rest of mankind.[1]

Thus Condorcet held that the priesthood as an institution had exerted a twofold influence on human progress : it had advanced knowledge, yet diffused error : it had enriched science with fresh discoveries, yet plunged the multitude deeper in the abyss of ignorance and superstition. There can be little doubt that in these conclusions Condorcet exag-gerated both the intellectual attainments and the moral obliquity of the class of men whom he criticized : the great majority of priests in all ages have neither been such accomplished sages nor such cunning knaves as he imagined. Indeed, it is safe

[1] Condorcet, *Œuvres*, vi. pp. 35, 52-58, 375-378.

to say that his strong bias and vehement prejudices against religion have seriously warped his general view of the part which religious faith has played in human history. He had an eye only for the evil and suffering, doubtless incalculably great, which have been wrought by certain creeds, but he was blind to the spiritual comfort and consolation, the inspiring hopes, and the active beneficence which have flowed from other creeds, or even from different aspects of the same.

In his history of human error Condorcet has to some extent anticipated the theory of Max Müller that mythology springs from a disease of language. Primitive speech, he points out, is largely metaphorical because early man lacks words to express abstract ideas. In course of time the metaphorical language in which the priestly sages clothed, or veiled, certain simple natural truths was misapprehended by the vulgar, who understood the statements in their literal instead of their figurative sense, and thereby fell into extravagant errors and preposterous forms of superstition, believing, for example, that the heavenly bodies were men, animals, or monsters, whereas the priests, though they described them as such, well knew them to be nothing but stars.[1] In purely verbal misunderstandings of this sort Condorcet imagined almost all known religions to have taken their rise.[2] The theory is too shallow and too improbable to merit a serious refutation.

While Condorcet accepted the evidence which points to man's lowly origin and chequered career

---

[1] *Ibid.* pp. 56 *sq.*   [2] *Ibid.* p. 57.

in the past, he embraced with ardour, as we have seen, the doctrine of his indefinite perfectibility in the future ; indeed, he regarded perfectibility as a general law of nature applicable alike to all organic beings, whether animal or vegetable.[1] The last, and not the least interesting, part of his treatise is devoted to speculations on the course which humanity may be expected to follow hereafter in its progress towards that goal of absolute perfection which it will continually approach without ever actually reaching. He believed that the advance of medicine and of sanitary science would result in abolishing disease and prolonging human life indefinitely, though not for ever, so that death, when it comes, will be the effect either of accident or of simple exhaustion of the vital powers, which will be postponed to an ever remoter period.[2]   He held that the intellectual and moral faculties of man, like his physical constitution, are capable of limitless improvement, and that accordingly we may anticipate for humanity a steady growth in wisdom and virtue.[3]   He thought that with the progress at once of enlightenment and of popular government, men will come to regard war as the most fatal scourge and the most heinous of crimes.   Wars undertaken for dynastic reasons will be the first to disappear, and they will be followed into the limbo of the past by such wars as have their root in commercial rivalry and the selfish greed of gain.   Better instructed in the true principles of policy and ethics, the peoples will be drawn together in bonds of amity, they will invite others to share

[1] Condorcet, *Œuvres*, vi. pp.   [2] *Ibid*. pp. 272-275.
13, 272.   [3] *Ibid*. p. 275.

the advantages of nature and industry which they
themselves possess ; and thus the causes which now
excite, envenom, and perpetuate national hatred will
gradually vanish away and cease to furnish fruitful
pretexts for the madness of war.   United in a universal brotherhood, the nations will learn to see that
the sole means of guaranteeing their independence
is the formation of perpetual confederacies.[1]   Thus
Condorcet anticipated those ideas and aspirations
after a universal peace which in our time have
centred round the League of Nations at Geneva,
the new Jerusalem of war-weary humanity.

As one of the most powerful measures for hastening this happy consummation, our philosopher regarded the future extension of Free Trade throughout the world.   Trading corporations with exclu-
sive privileges, like the Dutch and English East
India Companies, will be things of the past, and
their counting-houses in foreign parts—those dens
of robbers where the plunder of oppressed nations
is heaped up to furnish the infamous minions of
government with the means of purchasing honours
and titles at home—will be replaced by colonies of
citizens who will diffuse among the benighted peoples
around them the light of reason and the principles
of liberty.   The cultivation of the sugar-cane, for
example, throughout the length and breadth of
Africa will destroy the shameful brigandage which,
in the form of the slave trade, corrupted and de-
populated that unhappy continent for centuries.[2]
Here again Condorcet has anticipated the march
of history by predicting the abolition of slavery

[1] *Ibid.* p. 265.   [2] *Ibid.* pp. 239-241.

throughout Africa, and foreshadowing the tutelage of the black continent under the aegis of the white.

With the entire freedom of commerce and industry, with the abolition of prohibitive laws, fiscal duties, and cumbersome legal formalities—the rusty and mouldering machinery of the past—inequalities of fortune will tend to disappear, and with them that social inequality in which Condorcet saw one of the chief evils of our existing civilization.[1] Of that social inequality he assigned three principal causes : first, inequality of wealth ; second, inequality of condition between those who inherit a competence and those who have to earn it by their labour ; and third, inequality of education.[2] As a means of reducing the disadvantage under which the working classes labour by comparison with those who have inherited a competence, Condorcet advocated a system of insurance whereby the savings of the workers would provide a fund for the payment of old-age pensions and the support of widows and orphans under age. Such a system of insurance, he thought, could be organized either by government or by private associations.[3] Here again Condorcet has anticipated the future, for the system of old-age pensions which he suggested has since been adopted in our own and other countries. The social inequality which springs from different degrees of education will in time be diminished by extending a measure of instruction to every member of the community, but it will not be carried to the same

---

[1] Condorcet, *Œuvres*, vi. pp. 245 *sq.*

[2] *Ibid.* pp. 244 *sq.*

[3] *Ibid.* pp. 246-248.

pitch for all : natural differences of ability between
man and man will still exist, but the superiority of
talent and learning will be for the advantage even
of those who do not share it, since they will benefit
by the teaching of their betters.[1]   Here again
Condorcet has anticipated the social legislation of
later times which in most civilized nations has
established systems of public education for all
members of the community.

Nobody, Condorcet says, has ever imagined that
the human mind could ever exhaust all the facts of
nature and all the means of measuring and analysing
them.   But as the facts multiply man will learn to
classify them and reduce them to wider and wider
generalizations ;   science and education will alike
progress by the improvement of technical methods
and the invention of instruments of greater and
greater precision ;   so that discoveries which at first
could only be made by men of the highest genius
will in time be made easily intelligible to persons of
ordinary capacity.   Thus, without assuming any
substantial increase of man's intellectual faculties,
we may yet reasonably anticipate that he will continue to advance in the path of knowledge by ever
fresh discoveries in the universe of which he seems
to form an insignificant particle.[2]

An expedient to which Condorcet looked for a
powerful impulse to the advancement of knowledge
was the institution of a universal language, which,
by expressing all shades of ideas with perfect exact-
ness, will lend a rigorous precision to knowledge
and render the acquisition of truth easy and the

[1] *Ibid.* pp. 248-250.   [2] *Ibid.* pp. 251-253, 269 *sq.*

commission of error almost impossible.[1]   Here,
again, Condorcet has so far anticipated the future
that modern times have witnessed several attempts
to construct a universal language, such as Volapuk
or Esperanto, though it might be too much to say
that the result has answered to his expectations.
Another instrument for the advancement of knowledge which Condorcet expected to yield great
results was the calculus of probabilities.   On this
subject he had long and deeply meditated,[2] and
now in his last work he expressed his deliberate
opinion that, applied to the social and moral sciences,
the calculus of probabilities was likely to prove
extremely fruitful by imparting to their conclusions
an almost mathematical degree of accuracy and
certitude, thus opening up to future generations a
source of enlightenment as inexhaustible as the
number of facts that can be submitted to its
operations.[3]

But, with all his bright vision of a blissful destiny
in store for our species, Condorcet did not shut his
eyes to some of the perilous reefs that loom ahead
of the ship of progress and threaten to wreck it. He
anticipated the problem which was afterwards raised
in an acuter and more insistent form by Malthus.
With the progress of science and industry the earth
will undoubtedly be made to yield a greater quantity
of food and hence to support a larger population ;
but can this increase of food and population go on
indefinitely ?   Must there not come a time when the

---

[1] Condorcet, *Œuvres*, vi. pp.   xxiv.
17 *sq.*, 261, 269, 270-272.   [3] Condorcet, *Œuvres*, vi. pp.
[2] Arago, *Biographie*, pp. xx.-   259-261.

increase of the inhabitants of the globe will exceed
the increase of the means of subsistence, with the
result either of widespread misery or of a reduction
of the population which in turn could not be effected
without severe suffering?   Thus it might be argued
that the perfectibility of the human species is strictly
limited by the amount of sustenance that can be
extracted from the earth, and that, though progress
may possibly reach that limit, it can never tran-
scend it.[1]

Plausible as the argument may sound, Condorcet
refused to admit it as conclusive.   He observed
that, should such a time ever come, it must necessarily be at a very distant date, and that in the long
interval mankind will infallibly have attained a
degree of knowledge and enlightenment of which
we at present can hardly form an idea.   Who, he
asked, would venture to predict what may one day
be done by art for the conversion of the elements into
substances fit for human use?[2]   And even though
population should ultimately reach a limit inexorably
set by Nature to life on this planet, Condorcet did
not despair; for, as he pointed out, men could meet
and evade the difficulty by limiting the production
of food to the amount necessary to maintain the
inhabitants of the earth in welfare and comfort, so
that there would be no need to reduce the surplus
population by the cruel and barbarous expedients
of abortion and infanticide.[3]   Could Condorcet have
foreseen that marvellous conquest of the air which
we of this generation have witnessed, he might

---

[1] *Ibid.* pp. 256-257.   [2] *Ibid.* p. 257.
                [3] *Ibid.* p. 258.

perhaps have dreamed of an aerial ark in which a remnant of mankind might yet escape from the foundering planet.

Having concluded his picture of the glorious future of humanity, advancing ceaselessly in the way of truth, of virtue, and of happiness, Condorcet falls at last into a strain of pensive, yet triumphant, meditation on the inward joy and peace which, in a sad and troubled world, the thought of that endless advance is fitted to afford to the mind of the philosopher. It consoles him, he says, for the errors, the wrongs, and the crimes with which the earth is still stained, and of which he himself is often the victim. It is in the contemplation of that picture that he receives the reward of his labours for the progress of reason and the defence of freedom. It is in such moments that he ventures to link his own efforts to the eternal chain of human destiny : it is then that he finds the true need of virtue in the accomplishment of a lasting good, which no vicissitudes of fortune can undo, and no revolution of time can reverse. This contemplation is for him an asylum whither the memory of his persecutors can never pursue him : it is there that, dwelling in thought with man reinstated in his rights and in the dignity of his nature, he forgets man as he is tortured and corrupted by greed, by envy, and by fear : it is there that he truly lives in the company of his peers in an elysium which his reason has created and which his love for humanity adorns with the purest delights.[1]

With these words, sounding like a benediction

[1] Condorcet, *Œuvres*, vi. pp. 275 *sq.*

or the last solemn roll of the organ in the fading
light of evening in some vast cathedral, Condorcet
brings his treatise to a close. Whatever may be
thought of the truth or falsehood of his speculations,
few will deny that the book does honour to the
character of the writer as a man and a friend of his
kind. Of it may be said, with at least equal justice,
what has been said of the great speech of Demos-
thenes " On the Crown ", that it " breathes the
spirit of that high philosophy which, whether
learned in the schools or from life, has consoled the
noblest of our kind in prisons and on scaffolds and
under every persecution of adverse fortune ". In
that high philosophy Condorcet sought and found
consolation in the clouded evening of his life.
When the defeated Roman general, fresh from the
dreadful field of Cannae, brought to the Senate
tidings of the greatest disaster that ever befell the
Roman arms, the Senate thanked him because he
had not despaired of the Republic. In the darkest
hour of his life and of the Revolution, to which he
had pinned all his hopes, Condorcet did not despair
of the future of France and of humanity. Let us
follow his example, and though the shadows of
night may seem to be gathering about us, let us
not despair of a brighter to-morrow for the world.

SPEECH ON
RECEIVING THE FREEDOM OF
THE CITY OF GLASGOW

(22ND APRIL 1932)

SPEECH ON RECEIVING THE FREEDOM
OF THE CITY OF GLASGOW

(22ND APRIL 1932)

My Lord Provost, Magistrates, and Members
of the Corporation, I am deeply sensible of the
great honour you do me by electing me a Freeman
of Glasgow, my native city, this ancient and re-
nowned seat of industry and commerce, of learning
and science. When I think of the famous men on
whom a similar honour has been bestowed in the
past, I am indeed proud to be deemed worthy of
being added to so illustrious a company, but at
the same time I am humbled by reflecting how far
the talents and the achievements of some of these
eminent men exceed my own. But without putting
myself for a moment in comparison with them I
accept with heartfelt gratitude the high distinction
you have conferred upon me. You have placed,
if I may say so, a civic crown on my brows, and
though it is invisible I shall wear it there to the
end of my days as a testimony of my fellow-citizens
that in their opinion I have not lived and worked
wholly in vain.

On this auspicious occasion my mind naturally

reverts to my dear and honoured parents, and I think of the joy and pride they would have felt if they could have lived to see this great honour bestowed on their son. They were both Glasgow people, my father by birth, and both he and my mother by long residence and manifold associations. Among those here assembled I know that there are some, and I hope that there are many, who remember both my father and mother with the respect and affection they deserved, though they died more than thirty years ago. As you know, my father, Daniel Frazer, was for long the leading partner of the firm of Frazer and Green, Chemists and Druggists in Buchanan Street. The firm was founded by his elder brother, Ninian Bannatyne Frazer, as far back as 1830, but my father joined it in his youth and continued in it till his death in 1900, though from 1892 onward he was laid aside by ill-health from active work, and lived in retirement with my mother at their home, Rowmore, on the Gareloch, Dumbartonshire.

In the ordinary course of events I might naturally have followed in my father's footsteps, joined him in his business, and succeeded to the management of it after his retirement. But I never had any taste nor, I fear, any ability for business, or indeed for any form of practical life. My tastes were always studious; my father early perceived it, and wisely allowed me to follow my bent without hindrance or even question. So I have always led the quiet uneventful life of a student. It is not a life about which there is much to say, but I have found it a very happy one, and I hope to lead it to the end.

I was born at Glasgow on the 1st of January 1854. My birthplace was a flat in the westernmost house of Brandon Place, at the corner of Blythswood Square. I have no recollection of the house, for from there my parents early removed to a ground-floor flat in Mansfield Place, off Bath Street, and from there again they flitted, as we say in Scotland, to an upper flat in La Belle Place, facing the West-End Park, in which as a child I played with my two sisters and brother. Afterwards my father bought a house in Elmbank Crescent (No. 39) which he owned and occupied at intervals for many years. It was from there that I attended my first school, Mr. Munsie's in Albany Place, a terrace facing Sauchiehall Street and adjoining the Woodlands Road. The terrace, I believe, still exists at the foot of Garnet Hill, though on the side of Sauchiehall Street it has been masked by a newer range of buildings. I remember Mr. Munsie as a red-faced dominie of the old school, but of his teaching I recollect nothing.

It was a happy day for us children when my father transferred his home to Helensburgh, where he had bought a little house with a garden (Glenlee, in Argyle Street) as a home for his mother, who spent the last years of her life there. In the garden, traversed by a picturesque burn purling at the foot of red sandstone cliffs, and in the beautiful natural surroundings of Helensburgh, situated at the mouth of the lovely Gareloch and looking across its calm water to the wooded peninsula of Roseneath, we children found more than a compensation for the somewhat grimy streets and lanes of the great city

in which too much of our childhood had hitherto
sought exercise and recreation. We now enjoyed
more of an open-air life, and doubtless our health
as well as our spirits benefited by the change. My
brother and I were put to school at Springfield
Academy under Mr. Harker, from which I passed
to Larchfield Academy, while my brother was sent
to a school of the Moravian Brethren at Neuwied
on the Rhine. My happiest school-days were those
which I spent at Larchfield. The excellent head-
master, Mr. Alexander Mackenzie, taught me the
rudiments of Greek and Latin and gave me the
taste for classical studies which I have retained ever
since. Among my schoolfellows at Larchfield was
Alexander Ure, afterwards Lord Strathclyde, President of the Court of Session, with whom I kept up
an intimate friendship to the end of his life. Another old Larchfield boy whom I should like to
mention in this place is our eminent citizen, Dr.
James Macfarlane.[1] We were not, indeed, contemporaries, for Dr. Macfarlane possesses the signal
advantage of being younger than me, but long after
we had both ceased to be boys I was so fortunate
as to make his acquaintance and to gain his friendship, and now we have common links in our attachment to the old school and in our happy memories
of the years we spent there in the heyday of our
youth.

From Larchfield I passed to Glasgow University, and I can never think without deep thankful-
ness of the education I received there, for it laid
the foundation of my whole subsequent career. I

[1] Now Sir James Macfarlane.

matriculated in November 1869. It was the last year of the old College in the High Street. The ancient building has long disappeared, but I remember it as a black and gloomy pile, of no particular architectural pretensions, backed on its eastern side by a spacious but rather dreary parade or recreation ground, which Scott has immortalized by making it the scene of the famous duel in *Rob Roy*. Next year (1870) the University was transferred to the fine site which it now occupies on the summit of Gilmore Hill, with its far view away to the south and its greensward sloping down to the banks of the Kelvin.

When I joined the University, more than sixty years ago, the course of study for the degree of Master of Arts was very different from what it is now. At present, as for many years past, I understand that every student is at liberty to choose from a variety of subjects the particular ones on which he desires to be examined ; but, however different may be the subjects which he has studied, and in which he passes the scrutiny of the examiners, every graduate receives indiscriminately the title of Master of Arts. In my time no option whatever was allowed to a student preparing for the Master's degree. Every one without exception had to study and satisfy the examiners in precisely the same subjects, which were Greek and Latin, Mathematics, Natural Philosophy (which meant Physics), Logic and Metaphysics, Moral Philosophy, and English Literature. It was an excellent scheme of a sound and liberal education, and I very much doubt if it could have been improved upon by being left to the choice of raw youths in their teens, as were many, if not most, of the students in those days. Certainly, for myself I have always been glad that in my sixteenth year I was allowed no discretion, but was shepherded into the fold of knowledge by wiser and more experienced heads than my own.

Among the professors at Glasgow University whose lectures I attended and whose teaching influenced me for life, there were two whom I wish to mention with special honour and gratitude. First and foremost was George Gilbert Ramsay, Professor of Humanity, that is, of Latin, as the subject was called in the days when Latin was the only gateway to humane learning. By his exquisite taste in literature and the innate charm of his delightful personality Ramsay was a most inspiring teacher. To him more than to any one else I owe the powerful impulse which directed the main current of my thoughts and studies for many years to the classics of antiquity. I have never regretted the direction thus given to my reading, for in my opinion the best preparation for a general study of man is the study of that splendid civilization of Greece and Rome from which our own civilization is directly derived.

The other professor at Glasgow University to whose teaching I am deeply indebted was John Veitch, Professor of Logic and Metaphysics, the pupil and biographer of the eminent philosopher, Sir William Hamilton. We may say that Veitch was the last representative of the line of purely Scottish philosophers, which, beginning with Hume, or rather with Hutcheson here at Glasgow, was carried on by Reid, Dugald Stewart, Brown, and Hamilton. The Scottish philosophers were the direct heirs and disciples of the great English philosophers, Locke and Berkeley, and like them were honourably distinguished by the clearness, simplicity, and literary finish with which they expounded their doctrines. They wrote like gentlemen in the language of polished society, and not like pedants in the uncouth jargon of the schools. The tradition was well maintained by Veitch, who, in accordance with an old Scottish custom, combined a Chair of Rhetoric with his Chair of Logic and Metaphysics. He was a man of true poetical feeling, and I well remember the quiet but deep enthusiasm with which he recited verses of Wordsworth and of the fine old Scottish ballad " Sir Patrick Spens ". His teaching made on my mind a profound impression which has never been worn out. It opened up an intellectual vista of which I had never dreamed before, and which has never since been wholly closed or obscured by later and very different studies.

Another item in the debt which I owe to Glasgow University ought not to be passed over even in this brief summary. It was my good fortune to attend the lectures of the great physicist, Sir William Thomson, afterwards Lord Kelvin. I cannot honestly affirm that he was a good teacher of elementary students like myself, whose difficulties he perhaps hardly appreciated ; but at least I carried away from his class a conception of the physical universe as regulated by exact and absolutely unvarying laws of nature expressible in mathematical formulas. The conception has been a settled principle of my thought ever since, and now in my old age I am not disposed to exchange it for that conception of the ultimate indeterminism of matter which appears to find favour with some modern physicists, though to me, perhaps in my ignorance, it seems to cut straight at the very root of science by eliminating causality and thereby implicitly denying the possibility of a rational explanation of the universe. I am unhappily no physicist, and I speak on the subject with all due diffidence; but I ventured lately to submit this opinion of mine to two distinguished French physicists and mathematicians in Paris, and was glad to find that they both cordially agreed with me.

At Glasgow University I thought of competing for the Snell Exhibition, which, if I had won it, would have carried me to Balliol College, Oxford, as it has carried many other Scotchmen before and since, including Adam Smith, one of the greatest glories of Glasgow and of Scotland. But as a strictly orthodox Presbyterian my father looked on the High Church tendencies of Oxford with grave mistrust, and fearing to expose me to the contagion he sent me to Cambridge instead. So in December 1873 I competed for an Entrance Scholarship at Trinity College, Cambridge, and being fortunate enough to gain it I entered as a student at Trinity in the following autumn. Thenceforth Trinity has been the centre round which all my studies, and most of my life, have gravitated till now. I may say that the great College has been the sun about which my microscopic planet has revolved, and, I hope, will continue to revolve till its glow-worm lamp goes out for ever. But that lamp, as I have indicated, was lit long ago here in Glasgow, from which I carried it with me to Cambridge.

On the course of my studies at Cambridge I must be brief, for I have already taxed your patience too long. My Scholarship at Trinity College was followed in 1879 by a Fellowship on the same noble foundation. The Fellowship has since been thrice renewed by the College, and I now hold it for life. By providing me with leisure and a modest competence it has enabled me to pursue my studies without distraction or interruption, and so has laid the foundation of whatever I have done, or attempted to do, for the advancement of knowledge. I can never emphasize too strongly the deep debt of gratitude I owe to Trinity College for the steady support and encouragement it has given me in my work ever since the day, nearly sixty years ago, when I first had the happiness and good fortune to set foot within its gates.

Before I close you will perhaps bear with me yet a few moments while I try to explain how it has come about that for many years the trend of my studies has shifted more and more from classical antiquity to a more general study of man, in short to anthropology, as this branch of learning is commonly called. My interest in anthropology was first aroused by reading Tylor's great book, *Primitive Culture*, which traces in masterly outline the evolution of culture from savagery to civilization. To that epoch-making work my attention was originally drawn by my philosophic friend, the late Professor James Ward, but my interest in the subject might have remained purely passive and inert if it had not been for the influence of another Cambridge friend to whom I am under lifelong obligations, the wonderfully gifted and altogether admirable scholar and thinker, William Robertson Smith. After being expelled from his Chair in the Free Church College at Aberdeen on the supposed ground of heresy, he was welcomed at Cambridge, at first as Lord Almoner's Reader in Arabic, and afterwards as University Librarian and Professor of Arabic. When I had the great good fortune to attract his attention and gain his friendship in the eighties of last century he was engaged in editing the ninth edition of the *Encyclopædia Britannica*, and knowing my interest in anthropology, he asked me to write for it the two anthropological articles, " Taboo " and " Totemism ". I accepted the invitation, and the researches I made for these articles were the beginning of a systematic application to anthropology and especially to a study of the backward races of men whom we call savages and barbarians. My reason for concentrating my attention on savagery rather than on civilization was this. Civilization is extremely complex ; savagery is comparatively simple, and moreover it is undoubtedly the source from which all civilization has been ultimately derived by a slow process of evolution. It seemed to me therefore that if we are to understand the complex product we must begin by studying the simple elements out of which it has been gradually compounded ; in other words, we

must try to understand savagery before we can hope
fully to comprehend civilization. For a similar
reason in chemistry the study of inorganic bodies
must precede the study of organic bodies, because
inorganic bodies are comparatively simple, whereas
organic bodies are highly complex and are wholly
compounded out of the inorganic elements. Thus
the study of savagery is of primary importance for
the science of man. It is further of urgent necessity at the present moment because everywhere the
boundaries of existing savagery are rapidly shrinking under the advance of civilization, and before
many years the savages will either have disappeared
or be so transformed that they will cease to possess
any value as evidence of the early condition of mankind in the days that preceded the rise of history.

But still in many parts of the world savages
observe their ancient customs and preserve their
ancient traditions. These customs and traditions
are of priceless value as documents illustrating the
long past history of our species, and it is the duty
of civilized nations to collect and treasure these
documents before they are lost, as otherwise they
will soon be, for ever. Anthropologists are aware
of the duty incumbent on them and are making
haste to discharge it before it is too late. The
Universities of Oxford, Cambridge, London, and
Paris have now men actively engaged in reaping
the anthropological harvest in fields that have been
too long white to the sickle. Why should not
Glasgow send out her reapers into these autumn
fields to gather golden sheaves before the winter
comes, when the harvest will be over and done,

not for one year only, but for all eternity? The merchants of Glasgow sit here at the gateway of the sea ; their ships go forth to all the ends of the earth and return laden with riches of many sorts. Why should they not bring back with them, from far savage lands, treasures of knowledge in the shape of records that will serve to enlighten future ages for all time on the slow and painful progress of humanity from its rude beginnings to that happier state which we confidently anticipate for our descendants?

My Lord Provost, Magistrates, and Members of the Corporation, I thank you once more from my heart for the great honour you have done me to-day, and for the very beautiful casket which commemorates that honour. I need hardly assure you that the casket, with its memories, will be treasured by me and as a precious heirloom by those who come after me.

MEMORIES OF MY PARENTS

VIII

MEMORIES OF MY PARENTS

WHEN a man receives the freedom of a city he may
naturally be expected, in returning thanks, to give
some account of himself and of his relation to the
city which has so highly honoured him. In my
Speech on the reception of the freedom of the city
of Glasgow I endeavoured to comply with this
reasonable expectation without, I hope, being unduly
egotistical in my reminiscences. But filial piety
prompts me to supplement with some further details
the little I said in that Speech about my dear and
honoured parents. For to their wise and tender upbringing I owe in great measure any success that
may have attended me in life. I say their tender
and wise upbringing, for I do not remember a single
occasion on which any of us four children, my two
sisters, my brother, and myself, were ever punished
by our parents. Indeed they had no occasion to
punish us, for we were dutiful and obedient children
who never dreamed of questioning their authority
or thwarting their wishes.

In a world in which there is so much evil we can
help the cause of virtue by prolonging the memory
of good men and women, who have themselves left
no permanent record of their earthly pilgrimage and

might otherwise be lost in the undistinguished crowd of the nameless and forgotten dead. That must be my justification for attempting to call up some dear and vanished figures from the shadowy past.

My father was a man of the most sterling character and the strictest integrity, respected by all who knew him, kind and courteous to every one without distinction of rank or station. On politics and religion he held strong and decided opinions in which he never wavered. In politics he was an ardent Liberal and a warm admirer of Mr. Gladstone. In religion he was a simple and devout Christian of unquestioning orthodoxy, who accepted the Bible in its literal sense as the inspired and infallible Word of God. In ecclesiastical matters he was a staunch Presbyterian and Free Churchman, with a large circle of clerical friends who were always welcome visitors to his house. In our household family worship formed part of the daily routine ; when my father conducted it, as he usually did, he always read a portion of Scripture without comment and prayed extempore, the whole family and the servants kneeling devoutly. The Sabbath was observed by us with the usual restrictions traditional in Scottish households. We never walked out of the house or the garden except to go to Church twice a day in the morning and afternoon, for the modern practice of holding the second service in the evening had not been introduced into Scotland in my youth. In the evening we children sang hymns at our mother's knee, she leading us, for she had a much better musical ear than any of her offspring. Later in the evening our father read to us a good or edifying book. Among the volumes to which I listened I seem to remember *The Fairchild Family*, Thomson's *The Land and the Book*, and Bunyan's *Holy War*. Our own reading was confined to pious or otherwise suitable books or magazines, among which *The Sunday at Home* was perhaps the principal favourite. We learned the Shorter Catechism by heart, and accepted its teaching without question as the standard of orthodoxy. I never found this observance of the Sabbath irksome or wearisome. On the contrary, I look back to those peaceful Sabbath days with something like fond regret, and the sound of Sabbath bells, even in a foreign land, still touches a deep chord in my heart.

I should add that though both my father and mother were deeply and sincerely pious they never made a parade of their religion ; they neither talked of it themselves nor encouraged us children to do so ; the subject was too sacred for common conversation.

In his personal tastes and habits my father was simple and abstemious without being austere. He usually took a glass of sherry at dinner, and whenever he entertained friends at his table, as he did not unfrequently, wine was always provided for them. But he never smoked and he disliked the habit of smoking in others. Within my recollection he played no games and indulged in no outdoor pastimes beyond taking a general interest in his garden. His chief recreations were reading and photography. Of his photography we retain many specimens, chiefly portraits of the family and of friends. Although he never acquired any foreign language, he collected a good library of English

K

literature which I inherited from him. He had a catalogue of his library made and privately printed. Among his books was, I think, a complete set of Sir Walter Scott's works, including what is called the author's favourite edition of the Waverley Novels. When the first popular edition of the Waverley Novels was published in the sixties of last century my father presented the volumes to me as they appeared, and I read them from first to last with keen enjoyment. He possessed fine illustrated editions of *Don Quixote* and Lane's translation of *The Arabian Nights*, and these too I eagerly devoured. In his library there was also a fine edition of Moore's *Lalla Rookh*, which I read with youthful enthusiasm, reciting the verses aloud to the accompaniment of an old lute or guitar. Among his books, the *Tales of the Covenanters* and Wilson's *Tales of the Borders* served to kindle or nurse the fires of piety and patriotism in my Scottish heart. Of my father's own taste in literature I can say but little, for he was not given to speaking much about it, but he was a great admirer of the writings of Hugh Miller, the Scottish geologist, he enjoyed *The Recreations of Christopher North* (Professor Wilson), and I remember his commending Green's *Short History of the English People*. His theological interests were attested by a complete edition of the works of Calvin in a handsome English translation. He regularly took in *Blackwood's Magazine* and the *Edinburgh Review*, of which he possessed complete sets to the date of his death. Not content with being merely a reader, my father made at least two modest attempts at authorship. He published a pamphlet called *Paper, Pens, and Ink*, in which he described the materials of writing and traced their history. Later he wrote and published a more substantial volume called *The Story of the Making of Buchanan Street* (Glasgow, 1885), that being the street of Glasgow in which his principal shop was situated, and in which the greater part of his active life was spent. But neither of these little works attracted much notice.

In his person my father was short, but not unduly so, and sturdily built. When the Volunteer movement was introduced in the sixties of last century he joined a Glasgow corps and was reckoned, if I remember aright, the strongest or one of the strongest of the men of his corps, judged by the test of holding his rifle for a time in a certain position. If I am not mistaken he had the honour of parading with his corps before Queen Victoria in a great review at Edinburgh, of which the family long retained a coloured print. But I cannot affirm that we could detect a portrait of our father in the serried ranks of the marching columns. Fortunately he never had to attest his strength and courage on a field of real warfare, but if the call had come to him I have no doubt but that he would have done his duty bravely. The modern conception of a patriot who refuses to defend his country had no place in my father's loyal and simple mind. With regard to the regiment to which he belonged, I recollect feeling a childish regret when the original green facings of the grey uniform were exchanged for what I thought a less becoming blue. In my father's face the most striking feature was his broad and lofty forehead ;

K 2

he has been thought to resemble the portrait statue
of the Spartan law-giver Lycurgus in the Vatican,
and from personal observation I can confirm the
comparison. Others thought that my father's
features resembled those of Herbert Spencer ; I
never saw that philosopher, but from his portraits
I should judge that the likeness was not very close.

A Glasgow newspaper, *The Bailie*, published an
excellent portrait of my father, in a series of portraits
of Glasgow worthies called " Men You Know ". I
may add that for many years my father was a
Justice of the Peace, but I do not remember his ever
acting in that capacity or alluding in conversation
to his judicial dignity ; for in that, as in every other
respect, he presented a marked contrast to the butt
of Shakespeare's wit, Mr. Justice Shallow. For a
number of years also my father, as an apothecary,
was a member of the Council of the Pharmaceutical
Society and used from time to time to attend the
meetings of the Council in the rooms of the Society
at Bloomsbury Square, London. It was a memorable event in his quiet life when the Council of the
Society paid him a visit at Levengrove, a large old-
fashioned country house at Dumbarton, which my
father occupied for some years from 1873 onwards,
for the sake of my mother's health, who had been
advised by the doctors not to live in Glasgow. The
house was pleasantly situated in its own grounds
looking across the mouth of the Leven to the tower-
ing rock of Dumbarton Castle, one of the three
great national fortresses which bestride the isthmus
between the Firth of Clyde and the Firth of Forth.
The two sister fortresses are Edinburgh Castle and

Stirling Castle, but, though both of them are superior in historical interest, neither of them equals Dumbarton Castle in natural strength and picturesque grandeur, rising as it does in sheer precipices from a dead flat. A memorial of the visit of the Council to Levengrove was a photograph of the honoured visitors with the members of the family among them.

After residing in these agreeable rural surroundings for about five years, during which he travelled daily to and from Glasgow on his business, my father removed once more to Glasgow, where he had bought and improved the westernmost house in Grosvenor Terrace, a handsome row of houses looking across the Great Western Road to the Botanic Gardens. This was the last house which he owned and occupied in Glasgow. From it he finally removed to Rowmore on the Gareloch, where he spent the last years of his life.

Among my father's personal friends I would make special mention of Mr. John William Burns of Kilmahew at Cardross in Dumbartonshire; for, having himself been educated at Trinity College, Cambridge, he persuaded my father to send me to compete for an entrance scholarship at that ancient and illustrious foundation, which has been the source of all my subsequent good fortune in life.

Of my father's paternal ancestry I know nothing. He was habitually silent on the subject, but my mother told me that he had formerly possessed a document tracing his pedigree through several generations, but that it perished in an accidental

fire. Among his books is a small volume on Highland customs published towards the beginning of
the nineteenth century by a clergyman named
Frazer, and I have a dim notion that the writer
was a kinsman of my father, but this is perhaps no
more than a surmise of my own. On the subject of
my father's maternal family I am better informed,
for his mother spent the last years of her life in his
house at Helensburgh. I well remember her as a
feeble little old lady of no very outstanding characteristics. Her maiden name was Isabella Bannatyne;
she was a native of Bute, perhaps of the little seaside
town of Port Bannatyne, for I remember being
taken on a visit to Port Bannatyne in my childhood.
Her two unmarried daughters, my aunts, also
shared the house with her at Helensburgh. The
elder of the sisters, Katherine or Aunt Kit, was somewhat hard-featured, perhaps with a disposition to
match; at least she showed little sympathy with us
children, and I fear that we felt little affection for
her. But she early disappeared from our lives, for,
as we learned later, she fell into a religious melancholy and had to live in retirement. Her younger
sister Grace, Aunt Grace, as we called her, was of a
very different temperament. Always bright, lively,
and good-humoured, she was a most kind and
affectionate aunt to us children; we never had a
harsh word from her and she loved to expend some
part of her very scanty means in making us little
presents. She was a member of the household till
her death in 1888; she is buried at Helensburgh.

My father's maternal kinsfolk the Bannatynes
appear to have had a predilection for the clerical

profession, for I knew three of them who were ministers of the Free Church. They were Mr. Ninian Bannatyne of Old Cumnock in Ayrshire, Mr. Alexander Bannatyne of Aberdeen, and Mr. Colin Bannatyne of Coulter in Lanarkshire. Of these the last and youngest distinguished himself as a leader of what was called the Wee Free Church at the time when that body refused to join the great majority of the Free Church in uniting with the United Presbyterians. Mr. Ninian Bannatyne had been a minister of the Established Church of Scotland before the Disruption of 1843, which resulted in the formation of the Free Church. The final separation of the two churches took place in the Assembly Hall at Edinburgh. When the dissident clergy, resigning their livings and casting themselves on Providence and the world, trooped out of the hall, the Moderator of the Assembly led the way and he was immediately followed by Mr. Ninian Bannatyne, for as private chaplain to the Marquis of Bute, then the Queen's representative at the Assembly, Mr. Bannatyne took precedence of all the other clergy. In our childhood my elder sister Christina and I paid a visit to the good old man at his manse in Old Cumnock, where he lived alone, for he never married. I remember him vividly as a courteous old gentleman of the ancient school with ruddy countenance, finely cut features, clean-shaven, and a most gracious and benign manner. He was the only man I ever knew who used to call my father by the familiar name of Dan, short for Daniel.

Another manse of a kinsman, to which in my boyhood I sometimes paid a happy visit, was at

Inverchaolain on Loch Striven. The old minister Mr. McTavish was related to my mother by marriage, for her eldest sister had married a Mr. McTavish about whom I shall have something more to say a little later on.   Loch Striven is the loneliest and least known of all the beautiful arms of the sea which branch out from the Firth of Clyde. For while villas, villages, and even towns stud the other shores of the Firth, and smart steamers churn their waters, trailing sooty flags of smoke behind them, no such habitations break the solitude of Loch Striven and no steamers plough its calm and silent surface.   Even at Inverchaolain there is, or at all events was in my boyhood, nothing but the manse and the little church to which, on Sabbath mornings, a handful of shepherds used to gather for divine worship from the neighbouring hills.   The whole scene breathes an atmosphere of pastoral peace and repose.   At the manse I found a congenial companion in the invalid son of the minister, Hunter McTavish by name, whom I afterwards visited in his retirement at Bridge of Allan ; and I made friends with two big dogs, a large deerhound and a ferocious-looking but really gentle bulldog. At the manse an old brass blunderbuss of an antique pattern looked odd in its peaceful surroundings.

My father's elder brother, James, was a master printer in a small way at Glasgow. I remember him as a gentle, kindly old man who took a great interest in steamboats, of which he even detected a prediction in one of the Hebrew prophets. For many years he published regularly time-tables for

VIII   MEMORIES OF MY PARENTS   141

steamboats and railways in Scotland. After his death the business was continued for a time by his eldest son, William. The younger son, Joseph, entered the ministry of the Free Church and held a charge on the south side of Glasgow till his death a few years ago. He lived unmarried with his sister, who survives him.

If every one who knew my father respected him, every one who knew my mother loved her, for she endeared herself to all by her sweet, gentle, and truly womanly nature. Cheerful and sociable, she was content to perform the simple duties and to enjoy the simple pleasures of domestic life surrounded by her family and friends; but with all her gentleness she was by no means destitute of spirit: she told me that whenever she heard military music she felt moved to rush out and plunge into the fray! For indeed in her quiet nature there was a vein of chivalry and romance. In religion she shared my father's child-like faith; on that sacred subject I cannot think that the shadow of doubt ever dimmed the clear surface of her mind or troubled her serene confidence in the merits of her Saviour. She died on the 16th of February 1899, while the snowdrops were in bloom in the garden, with her arms resting on the volumes of my *Pausanias*, which I had had the happiness of laying on her bed when they first appeared about a year before. My dear wife had then cut the pages of the volume for her with the kind thought of thus saving her some needless trouble, but she found that my mother would have preferred to cut the pages for herself, fingering and gloating over the volumes to the publication of which

she had looked forward for many years. They may
have been the last object on which her eyes rested at
death. Alas, I was not with her at the end.

Unlike my father, my mother loved to speak of
her family and ancestry, of which she was proud.
Her maiden name was Katherine Brown. Her
father was John Brown, son of Thomas Brown, by
Martha Bogle, daughter of George Bogle of Daldowie. Her mother's maiden name was Katherine
McCall; she was a daughter of George McCall, one
of the old " Virginia Dons ". The family names
that were oftenest on her lips were those of the
Browns, the Bogles, and the McCalls. Unfortunately I never made notes of her conversation and I
cannot now disentangle the various strains of her
ancestry, particularly the relation of the Browns to
the Bogles, but from what I gathered I think that
originally they were well-to-do Glasgow merchants,
trading with the West Indies or Virginia, some of
whom bought estates and lived on their land as
country gentry in the eighteenth and nineteenth
centuries. The estates of which she oftenest spoke
were Daldowie and Langside near Glasgow, and
Lanfine and Waterhaughs near Kilmarnock in Ayrshire. Of these estates Daldowie, pleasantly situated on the right bank of the Clyde about five miles
east of Glasgow, on the road to Bothwell, was held
by the Bogles and their descendants from 1724
onwards, while the estates of Langside and Lanfine
were acquired by the Browns at later dates. All of
these estates are described and their relation to my
mother's family mentioned in a book called *Old
Country Houses of the Old Glasgow Gentry*, which

was published at Glasgow in the seventies of last century.[1]

Of these estates the only one with which I was personally acquainted was Lanfine and Water-haughs in Ayrshire.   The last member of the family who owned it was my mother's cousin, Miss Martha Brown.   After the death of her brother Thomas in 1873 she renewed with my mother the friendly relations which had been broken off many years before at my mother's marriage ; thenceforward my elder sister Christina and I paid her an occasional visit at Lanfine, but my mother never revisited the ancestral home.   The house is a plain, old-fashioned country house of no great size, standing in its own large park with a long avenue leading down to the village of Newmilns and another avenue of equal length leading down to another village of which the name has escaped me.   Miss Martha Brown was a woman of strong common sense and some literary taste, which she showed in some letters that she wrote to me.   At her death she bequeathed the great bulk of the estate to various charities, with sub-stantial legacies to my two sisters, my brother, and myself.   The estate comprised about six thousand acres and was sold, I think, for something over a hundred and fifty thousand pounds.   My mother told me that originally the estate had been entailed, but that the entail was broken by Mr. Thomas Brown to disinherit a cousin of mine, Hugh McTavish, whose father had given mortal offence

[1] *The Old Country Houses of the Old Glasgow Gentry*. The first edition was published in 1870; the second edition in 1878. The publisher was James MacLehose. For the references to my mother's family see especially second edition, pp. 73-77 and pp. 159-161.

to Mr. Brown by injudiciously parading his son
as the heir of Lanfine.   I recollect having had a
passing glimpse of this Hugh McTavish in my
childhood at his father's house in Glasgow.   He was
a good deal older than I, and afterwards migrated
to the United States, fought in the American Civil
War, and fell at the battle of Bull Run.   We have a
photograph of him in his uniform and cocked hat ;
the expression of the face is stern and soldier-like.
His younger brother John, or Johnnie as we called
him, went to sea but ran away from his ship, and
after leading a wandering life disappeared somewhere in the Argentine.   Next to these two cousins
I believe that as my mother's eldest son I would have
been heir to the estate if the entail had not been
broken ;   certainly I acted as chief mourner, both
at the funeral of Mr. Thomas Brown in 1873 and of
Miss Martha Brown in 1897.   I have been told
that the tenants wept when they learnt that I was
not to be the laird, but they can hardly have
regretted me personally, for I never had any relations with them ;   they may indeed have regretted
the severance of the estate from the old family which
had owned the land for generations and had been,
it would seem, good landlords to them.

Among the family portraits dating from the
eighteenth century which are now in the possession
of my younger sister, there is one of a lady who by
her marriage with George Bogle, son of Robert
Bogle of Daldowie, in 1731, brought into our family
a strain of royal Stuart blood by two distinct lines
traced from James I. and James II. of Scotland,
and connected us, though remotely, with the noble

family of the Earls of Crawford and Balcarres.
She was a Miss Ann Sinclair, daughter of Sir John
Sinclair of Stevenston.   Curiously enough, through
another line of ancestry we mingle Cromwellian
with Stuart blood, being descended from a sister of
Oliver Cromwell.   This line is traced through Ann
Sinclair's mother, Martha Lockhart, who was a
daughter of Sir John Lockhart, Lord Castlehill, a
Lord of Session.   She succeeded her father in the
estates of Castlehill and Cambusnethan, and her
daughter Ann Sinclair was hence known in our
family as Lady Castlehill.   Martha Lockhart (Lady
Castlehill) was the widow of her cousin-german
Cromwell Lockhart, eldest son and successor of the
ambassador Sir William Lockhart, who married
Robina, daughter of John Shouster, by Anne, sister
of Oliver Cromwell.[1]   I may add that through the
Bogles we count kindred also with General Sir Ian
Hamilton.   While my sister Christina was alive he
visited her at Rowmore to inspect the family portraits
of our common ancestors the Bogles.

But though my mother's family can lay some
claim to an infusion of what is called blue blood,
none of them seems to have risen to high distinction
within the last two centuries or so, the only period
to which my knowledge of them extends.   At only
two points do they appear to have touched even
the fringe of history.   One of these points was the
Rebellion of 1745.   When the rebel army under
Prince Charles Edward was quartered at Glasgow my
mother's kinsman, George Bogle, the husband of

---

[1] *Old Country Houses of the Old Glasgow Gentry* (Glasgow, 1878),
pp. 74, 76.

Ann Sinclair and owner of the neighbouring estate
of Daldowie, received from the rebels a peremptory
requisition, demanding that a supply of provisions
for the use of the army should be sent in to the
Fishmarket at Glasgow before noon on the following
day, on pain of military execution to be immediately
done against him.   The demand seems to have been
complied with, for my kinsman received in return
a formal document commanding all the Prince's
officers to spare and protect the person and property
of Mr. George Bogle of Daldowie.   Both documents were long preserved in the family and are now
in my possession, but they are not beside me for
reference as I dictate ; they are printed at length in
the volume to which I here repeatedly make reference.[1]   The Protection is given in the name of
Charles, Prince of Wales, and is signed by John
Murray.   Both documents were exhibited at the
Glasgow Exhibition of 1911.   My mother preserved
a tradition of a visit of some of the officers of a
Highland regiment on this occasion to the family
residence at Daldowie.   The lady of the house was
serving out tea to some of these gallant men, and in
her agitation, having spilt some of the hot liquid on
their bare legs, she slapped the limbs by way of
rectifying her mistake.

The other point at which one of my mother's
kinsfolk emerged for a moment into the light of
history was in India.   He was George Bogle, son
of the George Bogle of Daldowie of whom I have
just spoken.   In 1774 he was sent by Warren

---

[1] *Old Country Houses of the Old Glasgow Gentry* (Glasgow, 1878),
p. 74.

Hastings on a mission to a Grand Lama in Tibet, though not to the Grand Lama of Lhassa. He was, I believe, the first Englishman to cross the Himalayas into Tibet. He accomplished his mission successfully and kept a journal which was preserved by the family and finally published for the Government about a century after his death under the editorship of Sir Clements Markham ; in the same volume the editor included the journal of another Englishman named Thomas Manning, the friend and correspondent of Charles Lamb, who had also travelled in Tibet but at a later date than Mr. Bogle.[1] As a token of his esteem and satisfaction the Grand Lama presented to Mr. Bogle a ring which was long treasured by the family at Lanfine. When the estate was sold the ring was submitted for valuation to a jeweller, who estimated its value at about tenpence, which seems to prove that the holy man of Tibet did not squander his treasure in profuse and indiscriminate liberality.

I may add that George Bogle of Daldowie, the father of the envoy to Tibet, would seem to have been a man of some local importance in his time, for he was thrice elected Lord Rector of the University of Glasgow in 1737, 1743, and 1747.[2] In his youth, with the approval of his father, he had studied Law and History at the University of Leyden. I possess an old note-book containing copies of many of his letters written from Leyden to his father, Robert Bogle, in the years 1725–

[1] *Narratives of the Mission of George Bogle to Tibet and of the Journey of Thomas Manning to Lhassa*, edited by Clements R. Markham (London, 1876).

[2] *Old Country Houses of the Old Glasgow Gentry* (Glasgow, 1878), p. 74.

1727. In these letters he mentions the professors whose lectures he attended and the books which he proposed to read, and incidentally he refers to his father's trade relations with Carolina and Greenland.

With some of my mother's other kinsfolk, the McCalls, I have had the good fortune to be personally acquainted. An unmarried aunt of my mother's, Miss Christina McCall, passed the last years of her life in my father's house at Glasgow and died there during our childhood. My mother was much attached to her and mourned her death. I remember her as a dignified and beautiful old lady of whom we children stood somewhat in awe, for she hardly unbent to us or took much notice of our childish ways. We have a coloured portrait of her which well preserves her fine features and stately bearing. Another of the McCalls, perhaps her brother, of whom we children heard a good deal but saw nothing, was Mr. Samuel McCall, or Uncle Sam, as we called him. He was a retired West India merchant, who was the first to build a villa at Shandon on what was then the lonely shore of the Gareloch. The house, named Linnburn, still stands but has since been enlarged. There he lived for years, but we children never visited him or it until the house had passed into other hands. We have a photograph of him taken from a pencil sketch made while he sat reading a newspaper.

Other McCalls with whom we counted cousinship and long maintained friendly relations were James McCall and his wife Eliza, and their kinsman Samuel McCall, a cheerful and lively bachelor. James and Samuel McCall were wine merchants in a good way of business in Glasgow. The son of James McCall, himself called James, studied at Christ's College, Cambridge, entered the ministry of the Episcopal Church of Scotland, and now holds a charge in the west of Glasgow. Our connexion with the McCalls is further attested by the baptismal names of my elder sister, Christina McCall, and my brother, Samuel McCall. My sister died unmarried in 1911. My brother married a Miss Ireland, and died in 1914, leaving a son, Ninian Bannatyne Frazer, who now holds a position of trust on a rubber estate in the Malay Peninsula. My younger sister, Isabella Katherine, married my good friend and trusted brother-in-law, John Edward Aloysius Steggall, with whom I was happy enough to make acquaintance some sixty years ago, when we were undergraduates together at Trinity College, Cambridge. Last year (1933) he celebrated his jubilee of fifty years as Professor of Mathematics at University College, Dundee, now part of St. Andrews University. He and my sister have two good and dutiful daughters, Katherine and Frances, named after their maternal and paternal grandmothers. Their only son John was an engineer by profession, but at the outbreak of the Great War he volunteered for the Navy, and died in the service of his country, going down with his ship, the *Invincible*, at the Battle of Jutland.

Of the houses which my parents occupied at various times two stand out in my memory as particularly dear and deserving of the sweet name of home. One was Glenlee, at Helensburgh, the other was Rowmore, on the Gareloch. Helensburgh is a clean, well-built little town, beautifully situated at the mouth of the lovely Gareloch ; southward it looks across the Firth of Clyde to the low blue hills of Greenock, about five miles away ; westward it has a nearer prospect of the wooded peninsula of Roseneath across the loch with the low green hills of Gareloch in the farther distance, and the rugged mountains of Loch Long rising above them on the western horizon. The town itself is laid out for the most part in gardens regularly intersected at right angles by straight roads or avenues usually bordered by grass and trees, with pleasant glimpses of the hills at their far ends. In the very heart of this town of gardens stands Glenlee. It is a little house with a veranda facing full south about which hops used to twine, and a sloping bank on which fuchsias with their red and purple blossoms used to grow. A burn winds through the garden, flowing for a part of its course over a pebbly bed at the foot of low red sandstone cliffs. At the back of the house it now carries a bridge, over which passes Argyle Street, a long, straight road, stretching east and west, from one end of Helensburgh to the other. But it was not so when my father bought Glenlee, somewhere about the middle of the nineteenth century. There was then no bridge over the burn and the ground was occupied by part of the garden of Glenlee, which thus interrupted and blocked Argyle Street, dividing it about the middle into an eastern and a western half. The first bridge over the burn was swept away in a flood caused by the bursting of a reservoir on the moor above the town. For some time afterwards the garden was strewed

with the scattered stones and wreckage of the falling
bridge.   We children had been playing on the banks
of the swollen stream a few minutes before the
catastrophe, but were saved from imminent death by
the hurried and timely intervention of a kind friend.
This was perhaps the nearest approach to an adven-
ture which I have had in my uneventful life.

The other house to which I have referred, Rowmore on the Gareloch, stands on an elevation at
Faslane Bay, about a mile from the head of the
loch.   From the house the garden slopes down to
the road, which here skirts the shore.   Southward
the prospect extends over the almost landlocked
loch, to the jutting and nearly meeting points of
Roseneath and Row ;   while westward you look
across the loch to the near green hills of Rahane and
Manbeg, with the loftier mountains of Loch Long
just peeping over their shoulder.   From the inner
corner of Faslane Bay, near a ruined chapel, a
rough road runs over the hill to the lonely Glen
Fruin, the Vale of Sorrow as it is called from a
brutal massacre perpetrated there by a Highland
clan towards the end of the seventeenth century.
The solitary road down the glen where some shaggy
Highland cattle graze used to be a favourite walk
of mine.   In such beautiful and interesting surroundings stands Rowmore.   It was the home of
my parents in their last years.   Both of them and
my beloved sister Christina died there, and they are
buried together in the churchyard at Row on the
Gareloch.   *Requiescant in pace.*